Pea

M000084706

Guide
to the
Colorado
Mountains

I-70 Skylines

TEXT AND PHOTOGRAPHY BY
JOE MILLIGAN

WESTCLIFFE PUBLISHERS

Published by: Westcliffe Publishers, Inc.
2650 South Zuni Street
Englewood, Colorado 80110–1145

Publisher:	John Fielder
Editors:	Cat Ohala, Mike Foster
Production Manager:	Harlene Finn
Cover and book design:	Joe Milligan

Publisher's Cataloging in Publication

Milligan, H. Joseph.
    Guide to the Colorado Mountains : I-70 skylines / text and
photography by Joe Milligan.
    p. cm. — (PeakFinders guides to the Colorado mountains ; 2)
    ISBN: 1-56579-191-6
    Includes index.

    1. Mountains—Colorado—Pictorial works. 2. Interstate 70—
Pictorial works. 3. Colorado—Description and travel. I. Title.
II. Title: I-70 skylines.

F774.3.M55 1997   917.8804'33
                                   QBI97–40282

For more information about other fine books and calendars from
Westcliffe Publishers, please contact your local bookstore or write,
call (303) 935-0900, or fax (303) 935-0903 for our free catalogue.

———————— For my wife, Marcy ————————
Without her dedication and help,
I would be stuck in some dead-end job
instead of writing and learning about the mountains
I enjoy so much.

Acknowledgments:
    The author would like to extend his humble appreciation and
thanks to the excellent librarians of the Colorado Historical Society
Library, the Western History Department of the Denver Public Library, the Colorado Springs Public Library, and to Colorado author
and mountaineer, Joseph D. Kramarsic.

Table of Contents

• 6 • SILVERTHORNE TO GLENWOOD SPRINGS

• 7 • GLENWOOD SPRINGS TO GRAND JUNCTION

See Your Name in Print!

If you have information that you think should be in this book, or, if you believe you have found an error, please write to the author in care of the publisher and enclose copies of any supporting documents or references, or contact the author via email at: (peakfinders@usa.net). If your information is used, you will be acknowledged in the next edition of the book.

Introduction

About this Book

- Use this book to tell family and friends about the mountains.
- Teach children Colorado history and geography.
- Provide entertaining road trips for out of town visitors.
- Satisfy *your* curiosity about the mountains.

Most of us have a strong curiosity about our surroundings. Being familiar with what's around us breeds satisfaction and understanding. Its almost a primordial urge to know our place in the world. Maybe it reaches far back in time to the flight or fight instinct. Men, in particular, seem to take pride in knowing where they are at all times, and where everything else is too!

In Colorado, knowing our surroundings includes the beautiful and dramatic Rocky Mountains—which dominate so much of the skyline throughout the state. It's somehow satisfying to know the peak names and their position. Once we know the name, its a naturally occurring thought to ponder the history that might be encapsulated in that name. When we finally know the name and something about the peak, our roots seem to grip a little tighter on our natural world.

Because they are there. PeakFinders guidebooks are dedicated to satisfying the curiosity and wonder we all have for the spectacular Colorado mountains. Intended for visitors and residents alike, these books will help you quickly identify mountain skylines and peaks throughout the state—from major roads to scenic overlooks and rural highways.

PeakFinders *Guide to the Colorado Mountains: I-70 Skylines* identifies the major mountains and landmarks of Colorado as seen from Interstate 70. It also gives you history, lore, and facts about the mountains, all in one easy-to-use volume.

With so many peaks in the Rocky Mountains, it can be difficult to identify each one. Topographic maps help, but most people do not know how to interpret these technical maps, which depict a *bird's-eye* view instead of a *roadside* view. Besides, it's impractical to carry the hundreds of topographic maps needed to chart Colorado's mountain ranges. In some cases, to reduce clutter in the photographs, I have chosen not to identify smaller features.

How to Use Your PeakFinder

This book is arranged by mile marker, the small green and white signs at mile intervals along the interstate, to make it convenient and easy to locate your position. Simply turn to the page of the book that reflects the mile marker closest to your current location.

At the top of each page is a photograph of the skyline, annotated with the names of the major mountains and landmarks that you can see from your current location. Simply match the mountain you see on the skyline to the mountain you see in the photograph. In some locations, a wide-angle panorama is followed by a page with a close-up photograph, in which more detail on individual mountain features can be identified.

Background information on selected mountains or landmarks is listed below the photographs. Information for individual mountains may be spread across many pages. Refer to the index for a list of each page on which a mountain appears.

Near the bottom of many pages is a map. It depicts your location (the gray circle on the map) and the direction in which to look. The following figure demonstrates how the map works. In this example you are at mile marker 237, just west of Denver. You are looking due west, toward the Continental Divide.

Be advised that you may see the same basic view for many miles. In other words, *the view at mile marker 237, to the west, may be very similar to the view you see from mile marker 250 or 220.* In this case, only one view and one mile marker are presented.

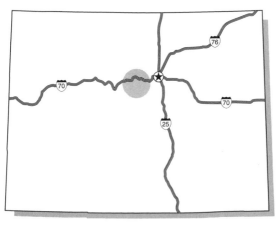

Mountain Locator Map

How to Identify Mountain Skylines

It can be very difficult to identify mountains. Although the mountains and landmarks are anchored in one position, they appear to move as your location changes. The skyline is not a cardboard cutout. It is a dynamic, complex view. The same mountain will look different from the north, from the west, or from the southeast.

As you drive along you may want to pull over and look behind you. Notice that the mountain that you passed 5 miles ago looks quite different now. The mountain's silhouette changes as your angle to it changes, and the elevation of your viewing location also influences the skyline.

One aid to identifying mountains is to visualize them and their neighbors in three dimensions. By identifying a prominent mountain feature such as a ridge, bump, or gully, you can shift that attribute left or right to help you find familiar patterns and shapes of the mountain. Once you can identify familiar shapes on the mountain, its usually quite easy to then recall the name.

Another helpful practice is to know and keep track of your orientation. Knowing if you are north, west, or southeast of a peak will assist you in tracking each mountain. Practice will increase your accuracy and allow you to identify readily the mountains you see on the skyline.

Locations for the photographs in this guide have been carefully selected to show the peaks and landmarks from a "middle point" or in their most characteristic view.

Visibility and Mountains

We all know that weather can affect visibility. When it is raining and snowing, visibility can be reduced to far less than a mile. The time of day is also a key element. Visibility is best early in the morning. As the day progresses, the contrast of the light becomes less and less as the sun climbs higher in the sky. Likewise, as the air temperature and humidity increase, the visibility decreases.

On a clear day in the early morning, you may be able to see more than 100 miles. Under poor conditions, it may be difficult to discern an object only a few miles away. When the conditions are very poor, you may be lucky to see an object only 1 mile away.

Tidbits—Throughout the book I have sprinkled pieces of additional information or related facts in what I call *tidbits*. When you see the compass rose symbol, like the one to the left, you have found a tidbit. Be sure to read it for additional interesting information.

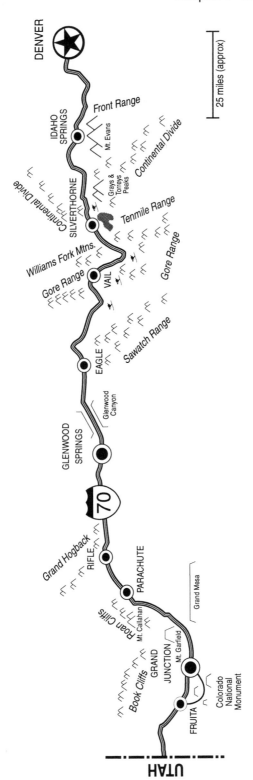

Interstate 70 from Denver, Colorado to the Utah Border

·2·

Geography of the Colorado Mountains

Traveling westward across Colorado's diverse terrain is a remarkable journey. Leaving the flat prairies of the high central plains, the visitor soon encounters the majestic peaks of the Rocky Mountains—the backbone of our continent and home to the Continental Divide. These shining mountains rise dramatically, marking an abrupt end to the Great Plains. More than 1,500 Colorado peaks rise above 12,000 feet. 54 reach above 14,000 feet.

Colorado Mountain Names

Colorado boasts more than 3,200 named summits. Thousands of unnamed summits, ridges, and high-points also exist within Colorado's borders.

The origin of geographic names is a rich area of study. Many names came from early explorers, cartographers, and settlers. Other names of geographic features honor prominent persons and local residents. Regrettably, most of the original Native American names for Colorado's geographic features are lost in history.

Many mountains have been known by more than one name. Explorers, settlers, and miners would bestow different names on the same peak, valley, or other feature. Over the years, this led to confusion and disorganization. In 1890, the United States Board on Geographic Names (BGN) was established to standardize geographic nomenclature. The BGN does not name anything itself. It merely accepts or rejects proposals for new names or changes to existing names based on its principles and policies. Primarily, the board rules on physical features and certain types of cultural features. However, the BGN will rule on any feature's name if asked to do so, or to settle disputes among individuals, groups, or organizations. The board also works closely with state name authorities and local governments toward the goal of placename standardization.

Geographic Definitions

What exactly is a mountain? For that matter, how is a hill different from a mountain? And who decides? There are no set standards for determining what is a mountain and what is a hill. The same can be said of other geographic terms, such as creek and river. A twist of an old proverb states: One person's hill is another person's mountain.

For some time, the BGN defined the difference between a hill and a mountain as 1,000 feet of local relief, but that definition fell into disuse by the early 1970s. Various agencies of the federal government may have definitions for their own specific applications, but there are no standards.

The United States Geological Survey (USGS) maintains a data base of all geographic names called the Geographic Names Information System (GNIS). In this data base are definitions for various classes of geographic features. The following classes are used in this book:

basin   A natural depression or relatively low area enclosed by higher land. Geographic features in this class include sink, pit, amphitheater, and cirque.

bench   An area of relatively level land on the flank of an elevation such as a hill, ridge, or mountain, where the slope of the land rises on one side and descends on the opposite side.

cliff   A very steep slope. Geographic features in this class include bluff, crag, precipice, head, headland, nose, palisade, promontory, rim, and rimrock.

gap   A low point or opening between hills or mountains, or in a ridge or mountain range. Geographic features in this group include pass, notch, water gap, wind gap, saddle, and col.

glacier   A body or stream of ice moving outward and down slope from an area of accumulation or an area of relatively permanent snow and ice on the top or side of a mountain or mountainous area. Geographic features include patch, snow patch, and ice field.

pillar   A vertical, often spire-shaped natural rock formation. Geographic features include pinnacle, chimney, monument, rock, and tower.

ridge   An elevation with a narrow, elongated crest that can be part of a hill or mountain. Geographic features in this class include rim, crest, cuesta, escarpment, hogback, and spur.

summit   A prominent elevation rising above the surrounding level of the earth's surface (not including ridges and ranges). Geographic features in this class include hill, mountain, knob, butte, berg, colina, cone, volcano, cumbre, dome, head, knoll, mesa, meseta, mound, mount, peak, rock, sugarloaf, table, bald cerro, and horn.

The Mountain Ranges of Colorado

The USGS defines a mountain range as a linear chain of hills or mountains that can be segmented into geologic or geographic units. Because a mountain range is viewed relative to its surroundings, you can consider the entire Rocky Mountains as a range, compared with the plains to the east and the deserts to the west. Within the Rocky Mountains are many groupings of mountains that are considered unique and linear ranges, such as the Front Range, the Sawatch Range, the Culebra Range, and the Sangre de Cristo Range. Sometimes the name does not even contain the word *range,* such as the Elk Mountains and the Wet Mountains, but a range is implied.

Many of the larger ranges can be further broken down into subranges or groupings of mountains and peaks, such as the Rampart Range, a subrange within the Front Range. Since there are no concrete parameters for segmenting ranges, this leads to some ranges having a local or common name, as well as an official name.

According to the USGS, there are more than seventy named mountain ranges in the great state of Colorado. As stated many groupings of hills and mountains can be divided into subranges. In this book, these subranges are referred to as groups.

The following list assigns a hierarchical order to the major Colorado ranges and subranges or groups. It includes USGS official names and local names that are, or, at one time were, in common usage.

Elk Mountains
   Anthracite Range
   Ruby Range
   West Elk Mountains
   Williams Mountains
Elkhead Mountains
   Sawtooth Range
   Williams Fork Mountains
Front Range
   Chicago Mountains
   Indian Peaks
   The Ironclads
   Kenosha Mountains
   Mummy Range
   Pikes Peak Massif
   Platte River Mountains
   Rampart Range
   Tarryall Mountains
Gore Range
Laramie Mountains
Medicine Bow Mountains
   Rawahs
Mosquito Range
Never Summer Mountains
Park Range

Rabbit Ears Range
Sangre de Cristo Mountains
   Culebra Range
   Spanish Peaks
   Wet Mountains
San Juan Mountains
   Chalk Mountains
   Grassy Mountains
   Grenadier Range
   La Garita Mountains
   La Plata Mountains
   Mesa Mountains
   Needle Mountains
   Rico Mountains
   West Needle Mountains
San Miguel Mountains
Sawatch Range
   Collegiate Peaks
   The Seven Hermits
Sierra Madre
Tenmile Range
Uinta Mountains
   O-wi-yu-kuts Mountains
Vasquez Mountains

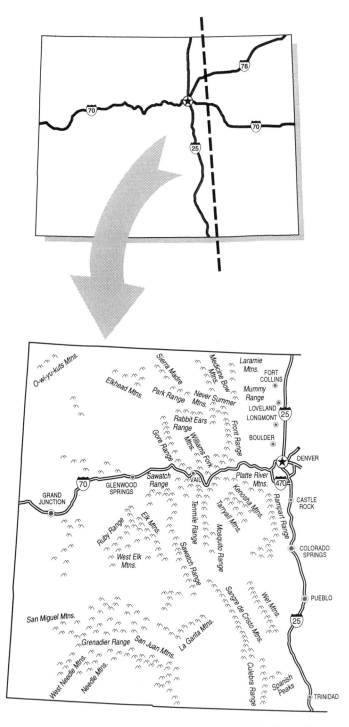

The Major Mountain Ranges of Colorado

•3•

Geology of the Colorado Mountains

The Rocky Mountains

The Rocky Mountains extend from above the Arctic Circle in Alaska south through Canada and the United States to Mexico. The Rockies contain many mountain ranges—more than one hundred distinct ranges in the United States alone. They comprise the longest chain of mountains in North America, at more than 3,000 miles.

Running along the ridge tops of the Rockies is the Continental Divide, where the Pacific and Atlantic watersheds separate. Water falling as rain or snow on the west side of the divide eventually makes its way to the Pacific Ocean. Water falling on the east side of the divide eventually makes its way to the Atlantic Ocean. The Continental Divide runs completely through North America.

Formation of the Rockies

The mountains we see in Colorado today are not the original Rocky Mountains. They are descendants of the original Rockies, which were known as the Ancestral Rocky Mountains. About 300 million years ago, when the continental plates were in collision, the Ancestral Rockies were uplifted thousands of feet. This was called the *Colorado orogeny.* Remnants of these early mountains can be found today along the Colorado Front Range. The tilted reddish sandstone rocks at the Garden of the Gods Park in Colorado Springs, the Red Rocks Park outside of Denver, and the Boulder Flatirons are some examples.

The Ancestral Rockies were eroded by wind, rain, and ice to nothing more than rolling hills. Much of the debris was deposited onto the high plains of the West. Then, about 65 million years ago, another uplift began the formation of the current Rocky Mountains. Called the *Laramide orogeny,* this uplift continued off and on until approximately 6 million years ago. This time was marked by periods of great erosion, volcanic eruptions, and regional uplifts.

The Ice Age and Glaciers

During the great Ice Ages that occurred from 6 million to 10,000 years ago, glaciers formed in the high mountain valleys. Glaciers are created as the annual snowfall exceeds the amount of snowmelt each year. Gradually, this unmelted snow compresses and turns to ice. As the years go by, the ice grows into huge glaciers, often many thousands of feet thick.

As gravity tugged at the Rocky Mountain glaciers, they moved slowly down the mountains, carving and gouging them, steepening their sides, and sculpting bowl-shaped depressions called *cirques.*

As the alpine glaciers moved downward, they carried rock and debris as they went. About 14,000 years ago, when the glaciers began to melt and recede up the mountainsides, they deposited the boulders and debris that they carried. The resulting low hills and ridges are called *glacial moraines* and can be found in many locations in Colorado.

The glaciers that occupied the Rocky Mountains enriched the landscape with breathtaking basins, high alpine valleys, and steep mountain peaks. Today in Colorado there are several permanent snowfields or "miniature" glaciers. Some of these have characteristics of larger glaciers, such as blue ice, crevasses, and deposit moraines along their margins and at their snout.

The Mountain Ecosystems

Within a day's drive, or a day's hike, you can visit the ecosystems of both the rolling plains and the frozen land of alpine tundra, more than 2 miles above sea level. Colorado truly is a diverse land of mountains and plains.

As you drive from plain to mountain top, you pass through five distinctive life zones, or ecosystems: grassland, foothill, montane, subalpine, and alpine ecosystems. For each 1,000 feet of elevation that you gain, the temperature drops by about 3°. Geographically, this is equivalent to driving 600 miles northward toward the Arctic Circle. Therefore, a trip from sunny Colorado Springs to the timberline on Pikes Peak, at an elevation of about 11,500 feet, is the same as driving north about 3,000 miles.

When driving in the high Colorado mountains, note that the ecosystems through which you pass share many similarities with those that you would see on a trip toward the Arctic. At the highest elevations, fragile tundra grows slowly, often taking twenty years to grow 1 inch. The summer is only about six to eight weeks long. The rest of the year is marked by snow, freezing temperatures, and strong winds.

·4·

East of Denver

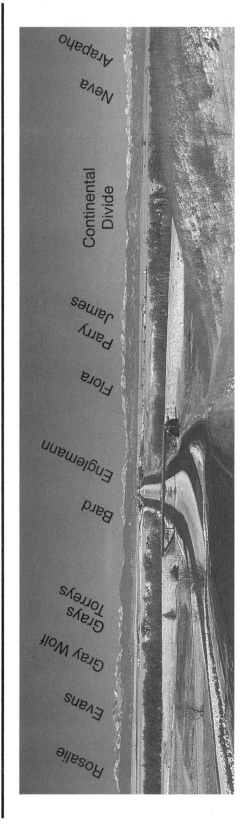

Rosalie • Evans • Gray Wolf • Grays Torreys • Bard Engelmann • Flora Parry James • Continental Divide • Neva Arapaho

After crossing the wide and barren plains on I-70, motorists are greeted with spectacular views of shining white peaks in the distance. Your first glimpse of the Rockies, at mile marker 355, is Pikes Peak, almost 85 miles away. As you head farther west, snow-capped peaks slowly materialize on the horizon. This panorama looks west from the rest stop located at exit 306, 70 miles east of the mountains.

Rosalie Peak—13,575 ft. Named for Rosalie Bierstadt.

Mount Evans—14,264 ft. The highest paved road in the U.S. goes to this summit.

Gray Wolf Mountain—13,602 ft. Named for the timberwolf.

Grays Peak—14,270 ft. Named for botanist Asa Gray (1810–1888).

Torreys Peak—14,267 ft. Named for botanist John Torrey (1796–1873).

Bard Peak—13,641 ft. Named for an early resident and doctor of Empire, Colorado.

Engelmann Peak—13,362 ft. Named for botanist George Engelmann (1809–1884).

Mount Flora—13,132 ft. Named for the Latin word *flora*, meaning "flowers."

Parry Peak—13,391 ft. Named for botanist Dr. Charles C. Parry (1823–1890).

James Peak—13,294 ft. Named for botanist Edwin James (1797–1861).

Continental Divide—13,294 ft. The ridge crest of the North American continent.

Mount Neva—12,814 ft. Honors an Arapaho who was a friend of Chief Niwot.

Arapaho Peaks—13,502 ft. Honors the Arapaho Indians of Colorado.

Interstate 76—If you are traveling east of Denver on I-76, you first see the Rockies from just west of Fort Morgan, Colorado, at mile marker 73.

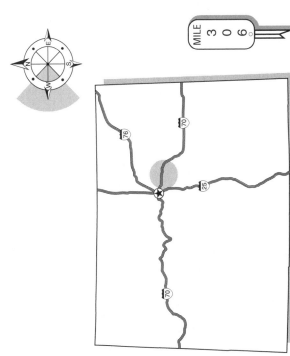

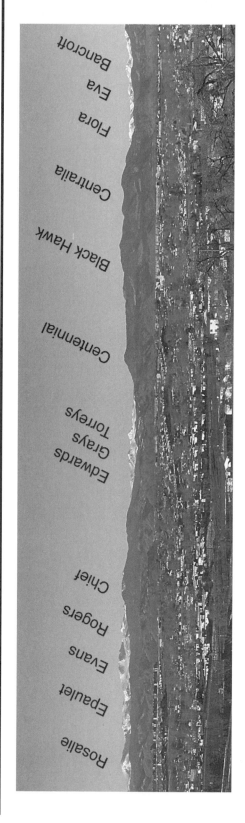

These mountains can be seen from the Denver metropolitan area. They are all part of the Colorado Front Range, which is so named because travelers from the east were greeted with this first view of the Rocky Mountains. These spectacular peaks rise majestically above the Great Plains and are about 30 miles west of Denver.

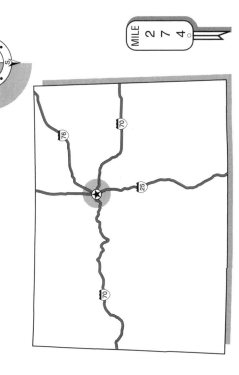

Rosalie Peak—13,575 ft. Named for Rosalie Bierstadt, wife of the great western painter Albert Bierstadt. Mr. Bierstadt has a peak named for him just west of Mt. Evans.

Epaulet Mountain—13,523 ft. So named because it is on the shoulder of Mt. Evans.

Mount Evans—14,264 ft. John Evans, second territorial governor of Colorado, had this peak named for him on his 81st birthday. It was formerly known as Rosalie Peak.

Rogers Peak—13,391 ft. Named for James Grafton Rogers (1883–1971).

Chief Mountain—11,709 ft. Named by the Hayden Survey in 1877.

Mount Edwards—13,850 ft. Named for the 1883 Colorado secretary of state.

Grays Peak—14,270 ft. Named for botanist Asa Gray (1810–1888).

Torreys Peak—14,267 ft. Named for botanist John Torrey (1796–1873).

Centennial Cone—8,679 ft.

Black Hawk Mountain—9,991 ft. Named for an early mining company and town.

Centralia Mountain—9,795 ft. Centralia was one of several names suggested by Congress in 1860 for the U. S. territory that eventually became Colorado.

Mount Flora—13,132 ft. Named for the Latin word *flora*, meaning "flowers."

Mount Eva—13,130 ft. Named for Eva Ferguson.

Mount Bancroft—13,250 ft. Named for Dr. F. J. Bancroft, an early settler of Denver.

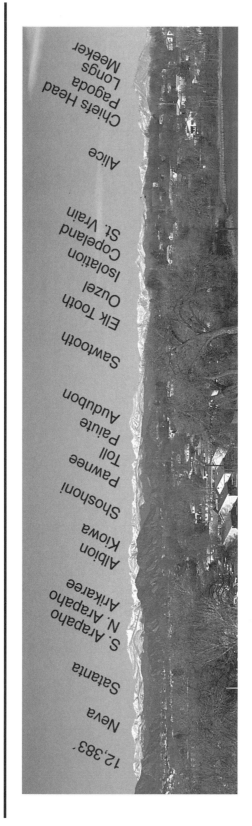

12,383'
Neva
Satanta
S. Arapaho
N. Arapaho
Arikaree
Albion
Kiowa
Shoshoni
Pawnee
Toll
Paiute
Audubon
Sawtooth
Elk Tooth
Ouzel
Isolation
Copeland
St. Vrain
Alice
Chiefs Head
Pagoda
Longs
Meeker

Many of the mountains due west of Denver are named for Native American tribes associated with Colorado. Consequently, this area of the Front Range is known as the Indian Peaks. To the northwest you can make out the huge profile of Longs Peak, the highest point in Rocky Mountain National Park. From Denver, you can see more than one hundred named mountain peaks!

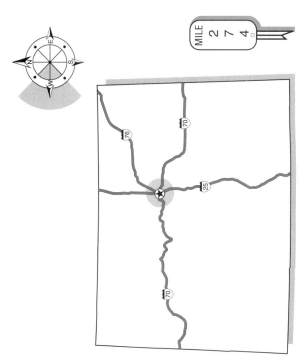

MILE
2
7
4

Unnamed 12,383—12,383 ft. This high-point has no name.

Mount Neva—12,814 ft. Named for an Arapaho Indian and friend of Chief Niwot.

Satanta Peak—11,979 ft. Named for a mighty Kiowa warrior, Satanta. "White Bear," as his name translates, fought hard to defend Kiowa lands from the white man. Captured and thrown into a Texas prison, he jumped to his death after three years of incarceration.

South Arapaho Peak—13,502 ft. The Arapaho are part of Algonquin Indian family.

North Arapaho Peak—13,502 ft. *Arapaho* means "our people."

Arikaree Peak—13,150 ft. Named for the Arikaree Indians. *Arikaree* means "horn."

Mount Albion—12,609 ft. Albion is a Celtic word meaning "snowy white" or "alp."

Kiowa Peak—13,276 ft. Named for an Indian tribe. *Kiowa* means "principal people."

Shoshoni Peak—12,967 ft. Named for the Shoshoni Native Americans.

Pawnee Peak—12,943 ft. Named to honor the Pawnee Indians who lived in eastern Colorado. The word Pawnee means "horn." Pawnees stiffened their hair with paint and fat, making it stand up like a horn, and dared their enemies to lift their scalps.

Mount Toll—12,979 ft. Named for Roger W. Toll (1883–1936), third superintendent of Rocky Mountain National Park. Toll promoted the building of Trail Ridge Road and attempted to expand the park by including the Indian Peaks area.

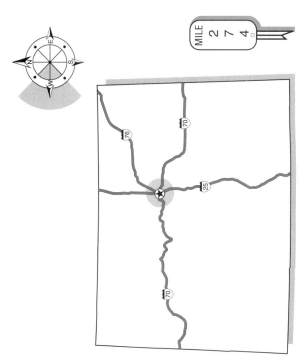

(continued on next page)

Chapter 4 • East of Denver

Paiute Peak—13,088 ft. Paiute means "true Ute" or "Water Ute."

Mount Audubon—13,223 ft. Named for the naturalist John James Audubon (1785-1851). The famous Audubon Society is named for him

Sawtooth Mountain—12,304 ft. Looking like the tooth of some gigantic saw blade, this peak is the eastern most point of the entire Continental Divide.

Elk Tooth—12,848 ft. So named because it resembles the shape of an elk's tooth. The Indian word for elk is *wapiti*.

Ouzel Peak—12,716 ft. Named after Ouzel Lake, and was once called Ouzel Lake Peak. Both of these features are named for the water ouzel, a bird commonly known as the water dipper which dives into streams in search of bugs.

Isolation Peak—13,118 ft. Named for its secluded location on the Continental Divide.

Mount Copeland—13,176 ft. Named for an early settler in Allenspark, Colorado. This peak has also been known as Rosa, Mount Mack, and Mount Tyndall.

St. Vrain Mountain—12,162 ft. Named after St. Vrain Creek, which in turn is named for Ceran St. Vrain (1802–1870). The sons of a noble French family,

Ceran and brother Marcellin were prominent figures in early Colorado history, amassing huge land holdings in the southern portion on the state.

Mount Alice—13,310 ft. The naming of this peak is lost in history.

Chiefs Head Peak—13,579 ft. The Arapahos called this peak "Head Mountain" for the outline of an Indian chief, dressed in a war bonnet, that can be seen on the side of the mountain.

Pagoda Mountain—13,497 ft. Named by an early Estes Park resident and artist who thought the peak looked like a pagoda, or Buddhist temple.

Longs Peak—14,255 ft. The highest point in Rocky Mountain National Park is named for Stephen H. Long (1784-1864), the leader of a western mapping expedition, who spotted the peak in 1820. Arapaho Indians were the first to climb the peak. They trapped eagles on the mountain's giant summit. The summit is so large, a football field could fit on the top of this peak.

Mount Meeker—13,911 ft. Named for Nathan Meeker (1814–1879), agriculturist and Indian agent who had a plan to transform the Northern Ute Indians into farmers. The plan failed miserably and he was killed in the Meeker Massacre in 1879.

·5·

Denver to Silverthorne

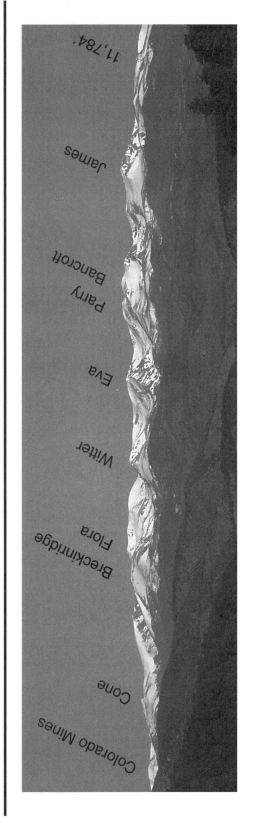

Colorado Mines
Cone
Breckinridge
Flora
Witter
Eva
Parry
Bancroft
James
11,784'

After making the long, steep climb from Denver, motorists are greeted with this spectacular view of the Continental Divide. Looking northwest, this view is seen from the Genesee exit, at mile marker 254. These mountains, part of the Front Range, are 23 miles away. A scenic overlook is located on the south side of the interstate. The north side has an overlook where a buffalo herd can be seen.

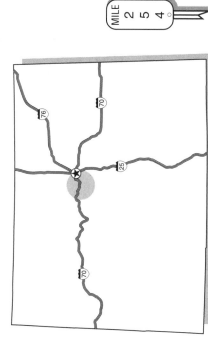

Colorado Mines Peak—12,493 ft. Formerly known as Mount Berthoud. Captain Edward L. Berthoud and Jim Bridger discovered Berthoud Pass, located just west of this peak, as a possible route across the Continental Divide for a Colorado railroad.

Cone Mountain—12,244 ft. Probably named for its conical shape.

Breckinridge Peak—12,889 ft. Named for John C. Breckinridge, who was Buchanan's vice-president. The town of Breckenridge changed the "i" to an "e" when it was discovered that Breckinridge was a southern sympathizer in the brewing Civil War.

Mount Flora—13,132 ft. Named for the Latin word *flora*, meaning "flowers".

Witter Peak—12,884 ft. Named for Daniel Witter of Denver.

Mount Eva—13,130 ft. Named for Eva Ferguson.

Parry Peak—13,391 ft. Named for Dr. Charles C. Parry (1823–1890), a great botanist. Parry named James Peak, Engelmann Peak, Grays Peak, and Torreys Peak for other botanists and naturalists who studied Colorado flora.

Mount Bancroft—13,250 ft. Named for Dr. F. J. Bancroft, an early settler of Denver.

James Peak—13,294 ft. Named for Edwin James (1797–1861), the prominent botanist and journalist on the Stephen H. Long expedition of 1820. James is credited with the first recorded ascent of a Colorado peak above 14,000 feet—Pikes Peak.

Unnamed 11,784—11,784 ft. No name has been applied to this peak.

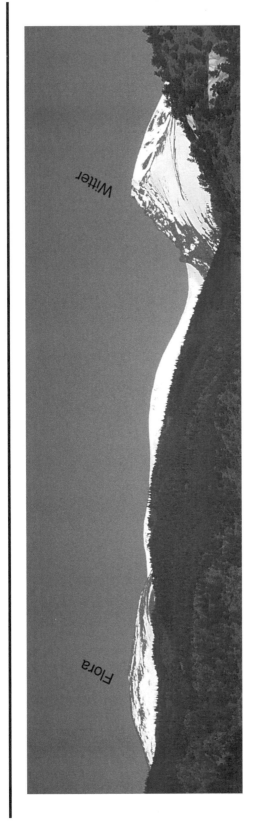

As you travel along this section of the I-70 corridor, most of the high and majestic mountains are hidden from view by the closer and lower hills. Occasionally, a glimpse of the surrounding snow-capped mountains appear. At mile marker 237 you can sneak a peek at two mountains located near the Continental Divide. The mountains are 9 miles to the northwest.

Mount Flora—13,132 ft. Historical documents suggest two explanations for the naming of this peak. One account says that Dr. Charles C. Parry, a botanist who spent time in Colorado from 1861 to 1872, named it *flora*, Latin for flower, in the summer of 1860 after collecting many species of wildflowers on the side of the peak.

The second explanation, proposed by Chauncey Thomas, an early Denver writer, indicates that the peak is named for his mother, Flora Sumner Thomas (1866–1943), the sister-in-law of W. N. Byers, founder of the *Rocky Mountain News*. Thomas states that Major John Wesley Powell, the great western explorer, stayed with Byers for some time. Powell started a Boy Scout camp at Berthoud Pass. While there, he named two mountains, one on each side of the pass, for Byers' wife Elizabeth, and her younger sister Flora. Thomas wrote the following prose about the peak and his desire to be buried on the mountain:

> Traveler—this summit rest—Behold the peaks—two oceans breast,
> Then on this grave lay you a stone—a mountain man sleeps here alone,
> When the time comes, I want to rest for eternity,
> Sleep on Berthoud Pass, in the mountains that are my religion.

At the age of 69, Thomas suffered a stroke. Three days later he took his own life with a Winchester rifle. Thomas was cremated and his ashes spread on the summit of Berthoud Pass and Mount Flora.

Witter Peak—12,884 ft. Named for Daniel Witter, a journalist and Denver businessman. Another source shows it is named for a man named Jacob Witter.

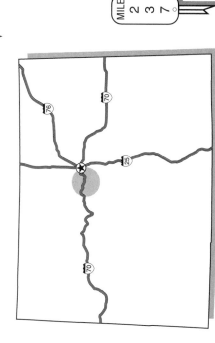

U.S. Highway 40 splits off from Interstate 70 at exit 232. U.S. 40 continues northwestward through the sleepy town of Empire climbs across the Continental Divide at Berthoud Pass, and continues on to Winter Park. In this photograph, the snow-capped peaks are about 9 miles away. Douglas Mountain, the small, rocky summit, is just west of the interstate.

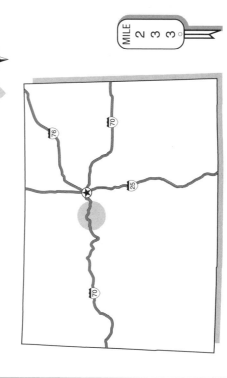

Republican Mountain—12,386 ft. Bob Ormes, noted Colorado mountaineer, reports that the origin of this mountain name comes from a woman who was disturbed by nearby Democrat Mountain. She climbed Republican Mountain, hauling along a flag pole, and raised "Old Glory" atop the peak.

Bard Peak—13,641 ft. Bard Peak and nearby Bard Creek, commemorate an early doctor from the town of Empire whose hobby was mineral collecting.

Robeson Peak—13,140 ft. This peak is probably named for Solomon Robeson, who came to Denver in 1859 and later made his home in Georgetown, Colorado. Robeson discovered more than a dozen mines near Clear Creek, many of them quite profitable.

Douglas Mountain—9,550 ft. Old timers say that this small mountain commemorates Stephen A. Douglas as "the little giant mountain." Douglas ran against Abe Lincoln in the 1860 presidential race. Douglas was only 5 feet 4 inches tall and earned the nickname "the Little Giant."

Engelmann Peak—13,362 ft. Botanist, Dr. C. C. Parry named this peak in 1861 to honor a colleague and distinguished naturalist, Dr. George Engelmann (1809–1884). A type of fir tree, the Engelmann spruce, also bears his name. Prior to receiving the name of Engelmann, the mountain was known as Crater Peak, an appropriate name because of the conspicuous north-facing cirque that can be seen from U.S. 40 on Berthoud Pass.

This panorama is seen by looking toward the northeast from the scenic pullout located at mile marker 226. At the base of these mountains lies the small, scenic village of Georgetown. At the Georgetown exit there is a wildlife viewing area where you can view the bighorn sheep that inhabit the hillsides to the north of the interstate. (Note: This scenic overlook is for eastbound traffic only.)

Saxon Mountain—11,546 ft. Named for the Anglo-Saxon mine located nearby. *Anglo-Saxon*s were Germanic people, Angles, Saxons, and Jutes, who settled in England over 1,500 years ago. In September 1962, Saxon Mountain was the site of a large search for an army deserter who was camped on the mountain. This peak was also known as Summit Mountain.

Woodchuck Peak—11,132 ft. This name shows up on maps as early as 1905.

Griffith Mountain—11,568 ft. Griffith Mountain is named for George and David Griffith. Brothers and Kentucky farmers, they came West during the 1859 gold rush. Together they founded the Griffith Mining District which later became known as George's Town and eventually as Georgetown. Georgetown was once known as the "Silver Queen of the Rockies" for the many silver mines located throughout the local mountains. In the canyon below the scenic pullout, you might hear the shrill whistle of a steam locomotive as the narrow-gauge train takes visitors up the Georgetown loop to Silver Plume.

Bighorn Sheep—The bighorn is a remarkable animal. Its agility on rocky slopes and cliffs is due to its cloven hooves with a soft-cushioned pad, which aids in balance. Bighorns have acute senses of smell and hearing, along with very sharp eyesight. During mating season the rams butt heads at speeds up to 40 miles per hour. Their clashing horns can be heard up to a mile away!

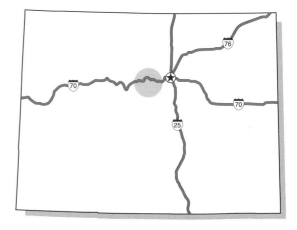

MILE
2
2
6

You have to look quickly to catch this view of Kelso, Grays, and Torreys peaks. Normally not visible from the I-70 corridor, they are only visible at the Bakerville exit. From this angle, most people mistake Kelso Mountain for Grays Peak. The summit of Grays Peak is almost 4 miles away. Kelso Mountain is about 1.5 miles closer. This view looks to the south. To the north is Bard Peak.

Sniktau

Baker

Torreys

Grays

Kelso

Ganley

Ganley Mountain—12,902 ft. Ganley Mountain may be named for a mine in operation around the turn of the century located south of Clear Creek.

Kelso Mountain—13,164 ft. Kelso Mountain is named for the first white man to ascend the peak—William Fletcher "Fletch" Kelso—who along with John Baker and others prospected for gold and silver in this area.

Grays Peak—14,270 ft. Grays Peak is the ninth highest peak in Colorado and the highest point on the Continental Divide in the United States or Canada. Grays and Torreys peaks are two of the easier 14,000-foot peaks to climb. From the Bakerville exit you can drive south up into Stevens Gulch for spectacular views of these majestic peaks. Stevens was another early miner in the area.

Torreys Peak—14,267 ft. Torreys Peak and its nearby neighbor Grays Peak were known as "The Ant Hills" by Native Americans. Charles Parry, distinguished botanist, named these peaks for his friends and colleagues Asa Gray (1810–1888) and John Torrey (1796–1873), also botanists. Asa Gray and John Torrey authored the book *Flora of North America.* They named many species of wild flowers found in the state. Prior to the name of Torrey, the peak was known as Irwin Mountain for Richard Irwin.

Baker Mountain—12,448 ft. Named for John Baker, an early prospector in the area.

Mount Sniktau—13,234 ft. Named for E. H. N. Patterson, a journalist whose nom de plume was *Sniktau,* an Indian word meaning "equal to any emergency."

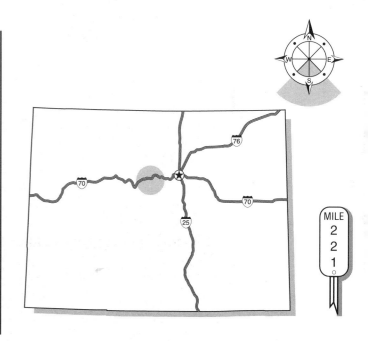

This photograph looks to the east from mile marker 219. Ganley Mountain is approximately 4 miles away. All of these mountains are part of the Colorado Front Range.

Pendleton Mountain—12,275 ft. Pendleton Mountain and a mine located on its flank commemorate the name of George H. Pendleton of Ohio, who was the vice presidential candidate in the 1864 presidential race. Pendleton was the running mate of George B. McClellan, commanding general of the Union Army during the early years of the Civil War. They were narrowly defeated by Abe Lincoln and Andrew Johnson, resulting in a second term of office for Lincoln. Located over the tops of these mountains is McClellan Mountain, which bears the name of the losing Democrat. In fact, Pendleton Mountain is actually a eastern subridge of McClellan Mountain, west of Leavenworth Mountain.

Ganley Mountain—12,902 ft. Ganley Mountain may be named for a mine in operation around the turn of the century located south of Clear Creek.

Baker Mountain—12,448 ft. Baker Mountain is named for John Baker who mined in the area together with William Kelso and Richard Irwin. Richard Irwin had his name bestowed on Torreys Peak (see previous page) before Parry christened it Torreys Peak. Locals called it Irwin for many years, but the new name of Torreys stuck and replaced Richard Irwin's name.

The Front Range—is a linear chain of mountains, consisting of nine subranges, that run in a north-south direction. They stretch from Colorado Springs, Colorado, to just north of Fort Collins, Colorado. At its widest point the range stretches from the edge of the Great Plains west to this area, about 45 miles wide and about 130 miles long.

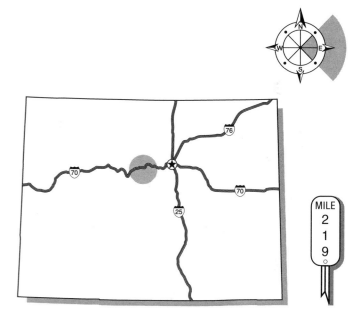

35

Mile marker 219 is only a few miles east of the Continental Divide, making the mountains seem to loom ever larger. Mount Bethel, the conspicuous mountain in the center of the panorama, is 2.5 miles to the west. Just to the south of Mount Trelease, behind Mount Bethel, is the Eisenhower Memorial Tunnel, which crosses under the Continental Divide.

Mount Trelease—12,477 ft. Mount Trelease is named for a Harvard botanist from St. Louis by the name of Trelease. Dr. C. C. Parry named this peak and four other great Colorado mountains for other naturalists.

Mount Bethel—12,705 ft. This symmetrically shaped mountain commemorates Ellsworth Bethel (1863–1925), a Denver high school botany teacher who is credited with the idea of naming Front Range peaks after the many tribes of Native Americans associated with Colorado history. While Bethel did not succeed with all of his names, he did secure approval from the United States Board on Geographic Names for seven tribal names on seven Front Range peaks. These include: Apache Peak, Arapaho Peaks, Arikaree Peak, Kiowa Peak, Navajo Peak, Ogalalla Peak, and Pawnee Peak. Shoshoni Peak, Paiute Peak, and, farther north, Commanche Peak, also honor Native American tribes associated with Colorado.

Bethel was a long-time member of the Colorado Mountain Club and also served on the Colorado Board on Geographic Names.

Pettingell Peak—13,553 ft. Pettingell is named in honor of Judge Jacob N. Pettingell, who served in Clear Creek County and Hot Sulphur Springs. Pettingell, a Boston-educated lawyer, came west in 1880 to recover from typhoid fever under instructions from his doctor. Pettingell was the editor and owner of the *Middle Park Times* newspaper which he later sold.

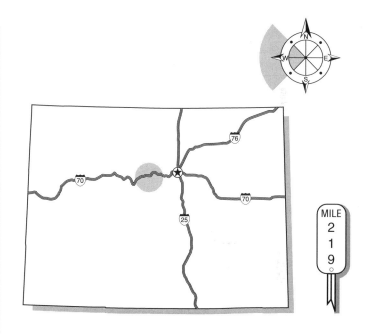

Only a few miles east of the Continental Divide, this mountain panorama looks to the southwest from mile marker 218. The mountains are only about 3 miles away.

Unnamed 12,276—12,276 ft.

Loveland Ski Area—Loveland Ski Area is a favorite location for Colorado residents. The neatly groomed chutes (or, in summer, bare stripes) on the sides of the mountains are ski runs. The rough and jagged gullies are avalanche chutes.

Continental Divide—12,701 ft. The Continental Divide runs along the roof of the Rockies. It separates the Pacific and Atlantic watersheds. Water falling as rain or snow will eventually make its way to the Pacific or Atlantic oceans, depending on which side of the divide it falls. The divide stretches through the continent from north to south, running approximately through the middle of the state of Colorado. The divide does not follow a straight line—it meanders, following the tops of the highest ridges and summits.

Mile Marker 215 Memorial—If you are traveling westbound on Interstate 70 near mile marker 215, just east of the Loveland Ski Area, you will see a large bronze memorial and a small white cross, which may be covered with flowers, dedicated to the Wichita State University football team. On the night of October 2, 1970, thirty-one team members and supporters lost their lives in a plane crash on the mountain above the memorial. The bronze plaque lists the names of those who died that tragic night. Miraculously, eleven passengers survived.

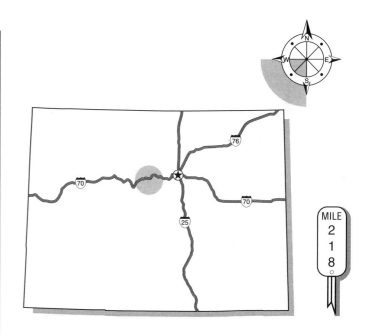

Look east from the Loveland Ski Area to view this panorama. Mount Bethel is 2 miles away and Mount Parnassus is 3 miles farther. Bard Peak is 5 miles away and Mount Sniktau looms, only 1.5 miles away.

Mount Bethel—12,705 ft. Mount Bethel is named for Ellsworth Bethel (1863–1925). Bethel was a true admirer and lover of the Colorado mountains.

Mount Machbeuf—12,805 ft. Named for Joseph P. Machbeuf, who established a Catholic mission at Denver in 1860.

Mount Parnassus—13,574 ft. Mount Parnassus receives its name from a mountain in Greece that was sacred to the Greek god Apollo and the Muses. Among his other titles, Apollo was the god of poetry. To this day, a poet is sometimes called a *Parnassian.*

Bard Peak—13,641 ft. Bard Peak and nearby Bard Creek commemorate a pioneering doctor from the town of Empire whose hobby was mineral collecting.

Mount Sniktau—13,234 ft. Mount Sniktau honors the energetic editor of the Georgetown newspaper, E. H. N. Patterson (1828–1880). Patterson, from Illinois, came west during the California gold rush where he learned how to mine. He returned to Illinois for a period of time and then came to Colorado. He became a journalist, writing for the Golden, Colorado, paper the *Western Mountaineer,* under the nom de plume of "Sniktau." Patterson later settled in Georgetown, Colorado, where he owned and edited the *Georgetown Miner* for many years. *Sniktau* is an Indian word meaning "equal to any emergency." Prior to receiving the name of Mount Sniktau, the mountain was known as "the Big Professor."

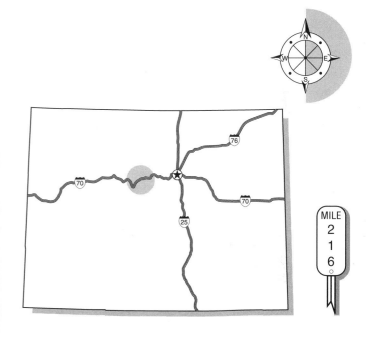

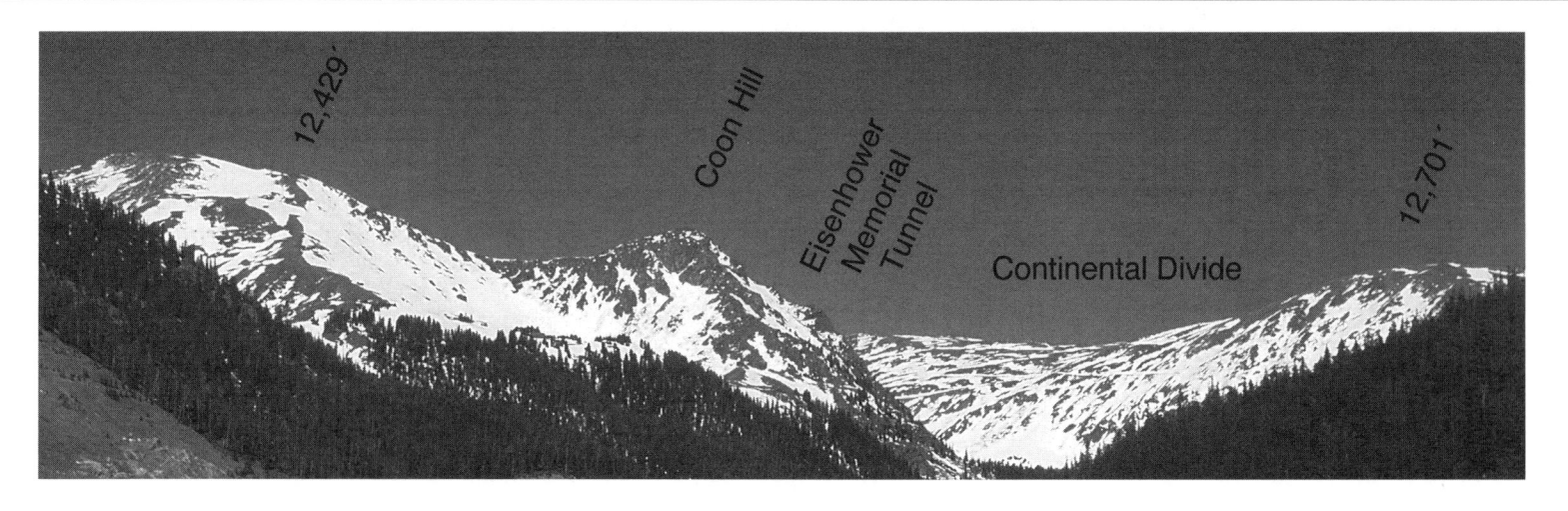

This panorama, from mile marker 211, is viewed by looking east to where the Eisenhower Memorial Tunnel crosses under the Continental Divide. The west portal of the tunnel is located just to the left of Coon Hill. The peaks to the south of the interstate have no names. The Divide is 2.5 miles east. Coon Hill is 2 miles away.

Unnamed 12,429—12,429 ft.

Coon Hill—12,757 ft. Probably named for that little masked varmint—the raccoon.

Eisenhower Memorial Tunnel—11,112 ft. The Eisenhower Memorial Tunnel is the highest automobile tunnel in the world. The tunnel is approximately 8,900 feet long.

Each tunnel has sixteen titanic-size fans, each one capable of moving more than 500,000 cubic feet of air per minute! The tiled walls and ceiling hide the fact that the tunnels are actually almost 50 feet tall and 40 feet wide. A pullout on the outside of each end of the tunnel allows for stopping, admiring the scenery, and access to little known restrooms.

This shortcut, under the Continental Divide, eliminates more than 9 miles of road travel that climbs across the sometimes treacherous 11,990-foot Loveland Pass. The tunnel was first known as the Straight Creek Tunnel for Straight Creek, which parallels this section of the interstate. The name was changed to the Eisenhower Memorial Tunnel by the Colorado legislature in 1972.

Continental Divide—12,701 ft. The Eisenhower Memorial Tunnel runs beneath this section of the Continental Divide. The divide separates the Pacific and Atlantic watersheds and stretches from Alaska to Mexico.

Unnamed 12,701—12,701 ft.

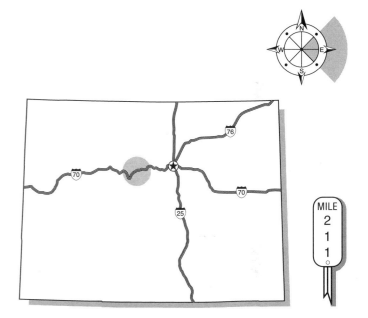

Buffalo

Holy Cross

Holy Cross Ridge

Whitney

Traveling westbound on Interstate 70, as you leave the west portal of the Eisenhower Tunnel, you are greeted with a spectacular panoramic view of the Tenmile Range, and portions of the Sawatch and Gore Ranges. Pages, 44 through 49 depict this beautiful panorama. Holy Cross Ridge is about 33 miles to the west.

Whitney Peak—13,271 ft. Named for W. D. Whitney, a Yale philologist. The name shows up on Hayden Survey maps in 1877.

Holy Cross Ridge—13,831 ft. This ridge received its name from Mount of the Holy Cross, located on the northern portion of the ridge. Holy Cross Ridge is about 5.5 miles long. The area was declared a national monument in 1929, but declining visitation, and a suspected crumbling of the right arm of the cross, caused this standing to be revoked in 1950. It still is a national shrine.

Mount of the Holy Cross—14,005 ft. Few people know that this famous mountain can be seen from Interstate 70. It is only visible within a short distance of mile marker 210. This mountain gained international fame in 1873 after noted photographer William Henry Jackson photographed the snowy cross from nearby Notch Mountain while traveling with the Hayden Survey. The cross is more than 1,500 feet tall and is visible when gullies and chutes on the mountainside fill with snow.

Buffalo Mountain—12,777 ft. This dramatic peak is a predominate landmark of the Frisco and Lake Dillon area, which is also known as the Blue River Valley. The large depression at the top of the mountain is called a *cirque*. A cirque is a bowl-shaped depression that is carved out by glacial action.

It's thought that the name Buffalo Mountain comes from the large humped shape of the mountain, which resembles the hump on a buffalo. Herds of buffalo once roamed the Blue River Valley.

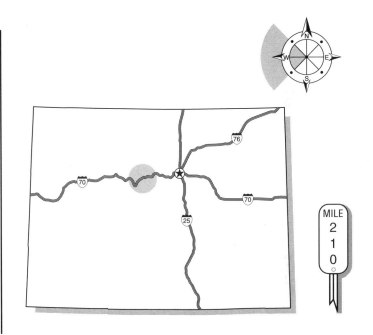

45

This photograph looks to the left of the previous photograph, a mile farther west toward the Blue River Valley. Buffalo Mountain looms nearby at a distance of 9 miles. Peak 1 is about 10 miles away. A spur of the Gore Range is 30 miles west. Vail Pass is 20 miles away via Interstate 70.

Tenmile Peak—12,933 ft. This peak gets its name from the Tenmile Range, which was once thought to have ten peaks in 10 miles along Miners Creek.

Peak 1—12,805 ft. The northernmost high peak in the Tenmile Range.

Vail Pass—10,666 ft. Once known as Black Gore Pass. Vail Pass honors Charles D. Vail, who was chief engineer of the Colorado highway department. Vail was known for his tenacity and tempestuous behavior. He ruled the highway department, and some say the state legislature as well, with an iron fist.

Uneva Peak—12,522 ft. Named for an early resident who owned a nearby dude ranch.

Gore Range—12,578 ft. The Gore Range takes its name from Sir St. George Gore, eighth baronet of Manor Gore, County Donegal, Ireland. You might say Gore represented the epitome of the wanton waste and rape of the early American West. From 1854 to 1857, Lord Gore and his elaborate entourage roamed the mountains and valleys of the West. Gore slaughtered every animal in sight, for "sport" alone, leaving the meat to rot. He drank from a silver goblet, ate in a carpeted linen tent, and always carried the necessities of a lord with him: including a bathtub, library, wine collection, pewter dishes, and a fur-lined privy seat. While Gore was on his three-year hunting trip in America, it's said he killed more than 2,000 buffalo, 1,600 elk and deer, more than 100 bears, and numerous fish and fowl, in the name of a "gentlemen's hunt."

Buffalo Mountain—12,777 ft. Named for the prominent "hump" of the mountain.

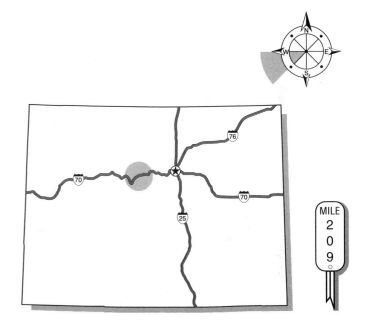

47

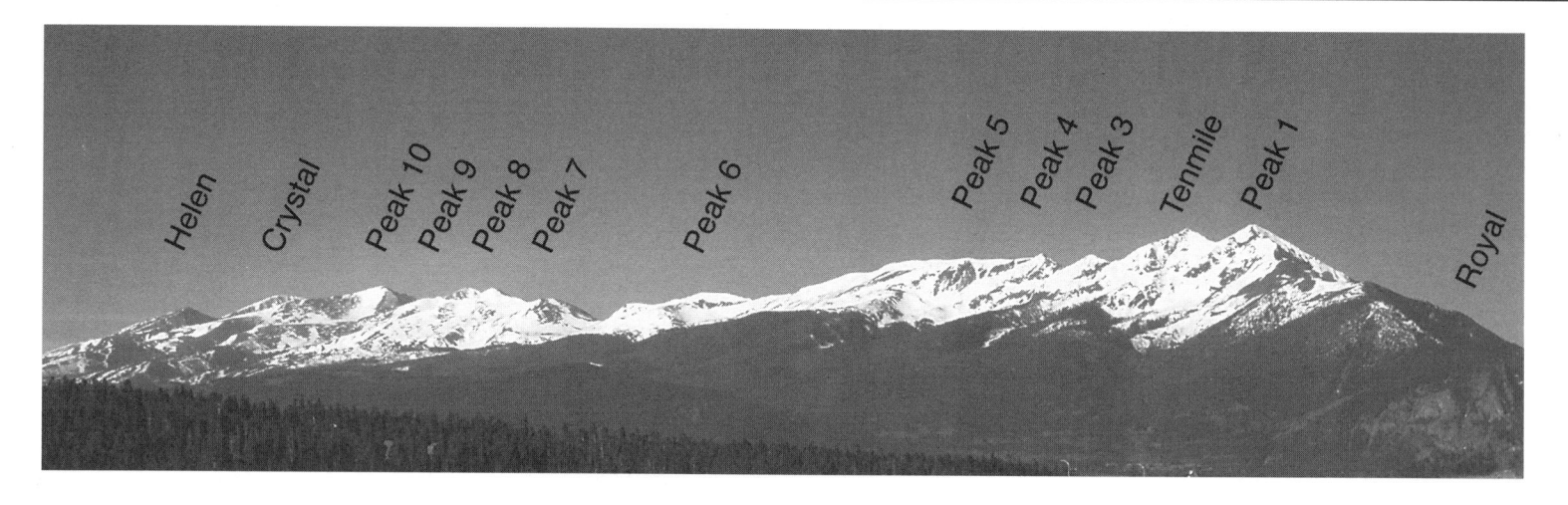

The majestic Tenmile Range rises above Lake Dillon and the town of Frisco. At the base of Peaks 8 through 10 is the old mining town of Breckenridge, now a thriving ski resort. During winter you can see the silken white trails that take skiers down the mountainsides. Peak 6, is 19 miles to the southwest.

Mount Helen—13,164 ft. Why this peak is so named could not be found.

Crystal Peak—13,852 ft. Most likely named for mineral deposits in the area.

Peak 10—13,633 ft. The tenth peak in the Tenmile Range.

Peak 9—13,195 ft. The ninth peak in the Tenmile Range.

Peak 8—12,987 ft. The eighth peak in the Tenmile Range.

Peak 7—12,665 ft. The seventh peak in the Tenmile Range.

Peak 6—12,573 ft. The sixth peak in the Tenmile Range.

Peak 5—12,855 ft. The fifth peak in the Tenmile Range.

Peak 4—12,866 ft. The fourth peak in the Tenmile Range.

Peak 3—12,676 ft. The third peak in the Tenmile Range.

Tenmile Peak—12,933 ft. Named for its position in the Tenmile Range. Early miners calculated the distance of this range at 10 miles long as they walked along the Miners Creek trail to and from their claims. They also surmised that the peaks in the range were about a mile apart, and consequently named them peaks 1 to 10. Today, we know the range is really 12 miles long and contains many other peaks as well.

Peak 1—12,805 ft. The first peak in the Tenmile Range.

Royal Mountain—10,502 ft. Royal Mountain is named after a successful mine.

Silverthorne to Glenwood Springs

From mile marker 204, view this panorama by looking northwest to Buffalo Mountain and Red Peak; Buffalo Mountain is 3.5 miles away. Red Peak is 4 miles northwest. These mountains are part of the southern section of the Gore Range.

Buffalo Mountain—12,777 ft. The long, prominent scar that is visible on the western side of the mountain is an avalanche scar. This large path was formed on February 22, 1986, when a week of heavy snows dumped more than five feet of fresh powder on the mountain. On that Saturday evening, a huge avalanche, starting near the summit of the peak, swept down the side of the mountain, clearing all the trees in its path. The avalanche was so large that the tumbling slabs of snow and ice created winds of up to 100 miles per hour, leveling trees that were 150 to 200 years old. This giant swath is two-thirds of a mile long and a quarter mile wide. Smaller avalanche scars can also be seen on the mountainside from earlier avalanches. Never underestimate the power of even a tiny snow slide. During an avalanche, the snow begins to melt from heat generated by friction. Once the avalanche stops, the snow re-freezes rapidly, trapping anything caught in its path in an icy grip similar to quick setting cement.

Red Peak—13,189 ft. Reddish mineral deposits in the rock of this mountain give it the red color—hence the name Red Peak. There were many mines located on Buffalo Mountain, Red Peak, and the surrounding mountains. Some of them reached almost to the summits of these great peaks, requiring the miners to haul heavy mining equipment and supplies up to their claims. Just out of sight, around the corner from Red Peak, are Silverthorne and East Thorn peaks.

Unnamed 12,885—12,885 ft. An eastern spur of Red Peak.

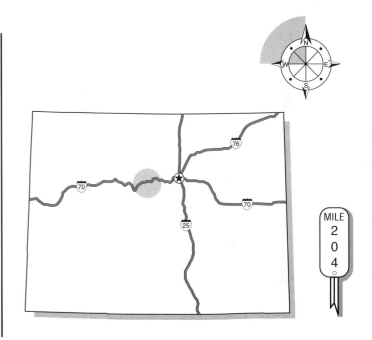

This 180-degree beautiful is from the scenic overlook located at mile marker 203. It overlooks the Dillon Reservoir and the Tenmile Range. In this segment, which looks to the southeast, the Front Range peaks of Grizzly, Torreys, and Grays can be seen 15 miles away.

Ptarmigan Peak—12,498 ft. Named for a bird that can live year-round above treeline. The ptarmigan grows feathers clear down to its feet which then act as small snowshoes. The bird's feathers turn pure white in the winter for camouflage.

Coon Hill—12,757 ft. Most likely named for the small, furry raccoon.

Tenderfoot Mountain—11,441 ft. *Tenderfoot* means a newcomer to outdoor life and may describe this mountain's easy climb, even for a tender-footed flatlander.

Grizzly Peak—13,427 ft. So named because grizzly bears were once quite common in the area. Grizzlies were sometimes spotted on the snowy summits of the high Colorado peaks!

Torreys Peak—14,267 ft. Named for New York botanist John Torrey (1796–1873).

Grays Peak—14,270 ft. Named for Harvard botanist, Asa Gray (1810–1888).

Porcupine Peak—11,803 ft. Named for the prickly little critter.

Independence Mountain—12,614 ft. This name denotes American patriotism.

Keystone Mountain—11,835 ft. Named after a railroad stop called Keystone.

Swan Mountain—10,796 ft. Named for the nearby Swan River.

Mount Guyot—13,370 ft. Named for Princeton geologist, Professor Arnold Guyot.

Bald Mountain—13,684 ft. A common name for peaks that rise above timberline.

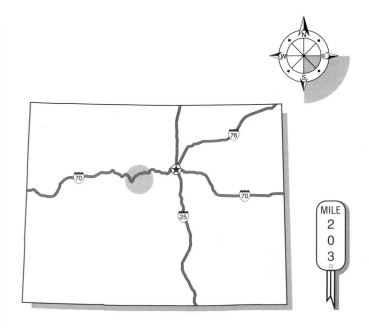

This panorama takes in the right half of the Dillon Reservoir scenic overlook located at mile marker 203. Mount Guyot and Bald Mountain are about 20 miles southeast. Tenmile Peak is about 7 miles south-southwest. Dillon Reservoir is a man-made lake that supplies water to the city of Denver.

Keystone Mountain—11,835 ft. A great ski resort is located on the side of this peak.

Swan Mountain—10,796 ft. Named after the Swan River.

Mount Guyot—13,370 ft. Both Guyot and Bald straddle the Continental Divide.

Bald Mountain—13,684 ft. An unimaginative name bestowed on many mountains.

Ophir Mountain—10,199 ft. *Ophir* is the biblical location of King Solomon's mines.

Peak 6—12,573 ft. The sixth peak in the Tenmile Range.

Peak 5—12,855 ft. The fifth peak in the Tenmile Range.

Peak 4—12,866 ft. The fourth peak in the Tenmile Range.

Peak 3—12,676 ft. The third peak in the Tenmile Range.

Tenmile Peak—12,933 ft. Tenmile Peak shares the name with the Tenmile Range. Tenmile Peak in located on the northern end of the range, which runs to the south.

Peak 1—12,805 ft. The first peak in the Tenmile Range.

Royal Mountain—10,502 ft. Named for a nearby mine.

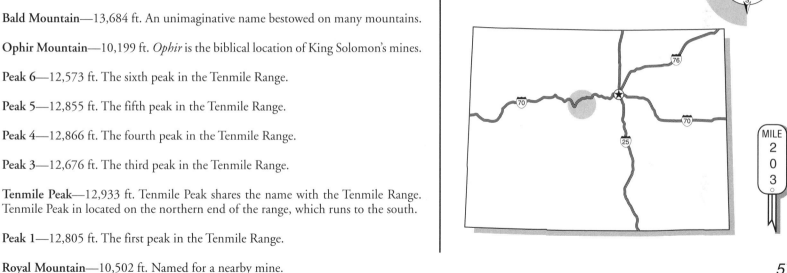

These two pictures are between mile marker 199 and mile marker 198 along Tenmile Canyon. They show Tenmile Peak and Peak 1 to the south. As you drive this portion of Interstate 70, you dip south and pass the west side of the Tenmile Range. The peaks loom above the road, only a little more than 1 mile away.

Tenmile Peak

Peak 1

Tenmile Peak—12,933 ft. Named for its position in the Tenmile Range. Early miners calculated the distance of this range at 10 miles long as they walked along the Miners Creek trail to and from their claims. They also surmised that the peaks in the range were about a mile apart, and consequently named them peaks 1 to 10.

Peak 1—12,805 ft. The first peak on the northern end of the Tenmile Range.

 What's in a name?—Many geologic and geographic features have been named. Maybe twice as many have not. Who decides? Early settlers, explorers, and map makers named the majority of geographic features. Local usage can sometimes override the original name, resulting in a new name or multiple names for the same feature. Also, legislative bodies have changed the names of mountains or "moved" the name to a different summit.

Categories of mountain names—Peak names fall into one of several categories which are listed below:

- Mountains named for individuals, groups, or institutions.
- Mountains named for animals.
- Mountains named for their shape or resemblance to something else.
- Mountains named after other geographic features.
- Mountains named after behaviors or events.
- Mountain names and meanings that have changed or been distorted over time.

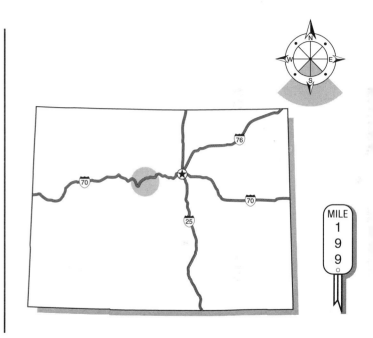

This panorama, at mile marker 197, looks southeast to some of the distinguished peaks along the southern section of the Tenmile Range. To the right of these peaks is a favorite ski spot—Copper Mountain. Peak 10 is 5.5 miles away, as is Crystal Peak. Pacific Peak is 6 miles to the south and Fletcher Mountain is 7.5 miles away.

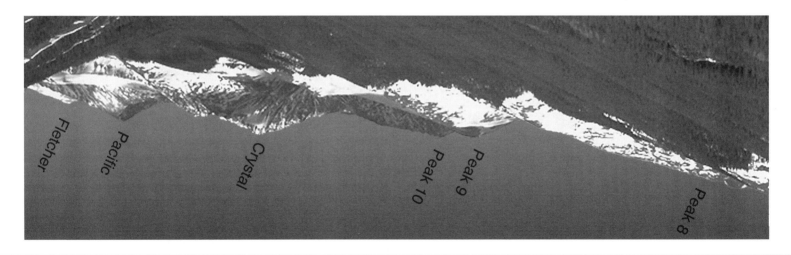

Peak 8—12,987 ft. The eighth peak in the Tenmile Range.

Peak 9—13,195 ft. The ninth peak in the Tenmile Range.

Peak 10—13,633 ft. The tenth peak in the Tenmile Range.

Crystal Peak—13,852 ft. Most likely named for mineral deposits in the area.

Pacific Peak—13,950 ft. Pacific Peak is so named because it sits just west of the Continental Divide. This means water falling on the peak will eventually make its way to the Pacific Ocean. Farther east, on the other side of the Continental Divide, is a mountain named Atlantic Peak. Water running off of it will eventually make its way to the Atlantic Ocean.

Fletcher Mountain—13,951 ft. Fletcher Mountain is named for a miner named Fletcher who had a claim nearby.

 The Tenmile Range—The Tenmile Range is 12 miles long and only about 6 miles wide. This small mountain range contains eighteen named summits including Quandary Peak which is more than 14,000 feet in elevation. The peaks include Tenmile Peak, Peak 1, peaks 3 through 10, Crystal Peak, Pacific Peak, Atlantic Peak, Fletcher Mountain, Wheeler Mountain, North Star Mountain, and Mount Helen.

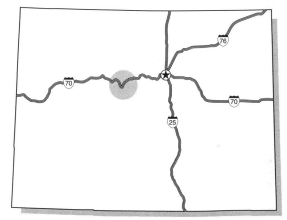

From mile marker 193, this panorama is viewed by looking east to the Tenmile Range. Peak 5 is 4.5 miles east, Peak 8 is 5.5 miles east, Copper Mountain is about 3 miles away and Union Mountain is 2.5 miles away. Copper Mountain and Union Peak are considered a part of the Gore Range and not the Tenmile Range.

Peak 5—12,855 ft. The fifth peak in the Tenmile Range.

Peak 6—12,573 ft. The sixth peak in the Tenmile Range.

Peak 7—12,665 ft. The seventh peak in the Tenmile Range.

Peak 8—12,987 ft. The eighth peak in the Tenmile Range.

Copper Mountain—12,441 ft. Miners once found low-grade copper ore on this mountain, hence the name. Today, the mineral mined here is Colorado champagne powder—light fluffy snow that attracts skiers from around the world.

Copper Mountain was one of three proposed locations in Colorado for the 1976 Winter Olympics. Sadly, the Olympics were hosted in Austria that year.

Union Mountain—12,313 ft. Since the name of this peak can be found on maps dating to at least 1896, the name probably refers to an early railroad station that was located nearby. The Burlington and Union Pacific Railway lines came together at this station.

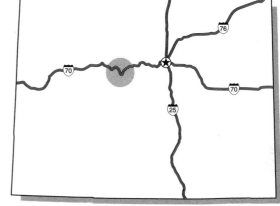

Did you know?—Colorado boasts more than 3,200 named summits. Thousands of unnamed summits, ridges, and high-points also exist within the Colorado borders.

Only a few miles from the summit of Vail Pass, this panorama at mile marker 192 is viewed by looking to the south. Copper Mountain is 4 miles away, Union Mountain is 4 miles south, and Jacque Peak is 5.5 miles away. All of these mountains are part of the Gore Range.

Copper Mountain—12,441 ft. Named for low-grade copper that is found on the mountain. Since it is low grade, no copper mining has ever been done on Copper Mountain.

Union Mountain—12,313 ft. Since the name of this peak can be found on maps dating to at least 1896, the name probably refers to an early railroad station that was located nearby. The Burlington and Union Pacific Railroad lines came together at this railway station.

Jacque Peak—13,205 ft. Jacque Peak is named for John W. Jacque, who owned a mine on the peak. There is also a Jacque Creek and a Jacque Gulch and Jacque Ridge.

Jacque Ridge—12,432 ft. Jacque Ridge is an extension or arm of Jacque Peak. There are two high-points on the ridge—12,432 feet and 12,596 feet.

Peaks in peril—Like much of the wilderness in our country, many of our mountains are in danger. The encroachment of commercial development and mining have had a profound impact on some peaks. Today, many of our mountains are being "loved to death." In increasing numbers, hikers, bikers, horseback riders, and motorists are traveling to the lofty heights of these beautiful mountains. Erosion, trash, and pollution are all by-products of visiting the peaks. Many of our high mountain areas are the headwaters for lakes and streams. Learn how to have minimal impact on these natural wonders, and protect the delicate mountain ecosystems.

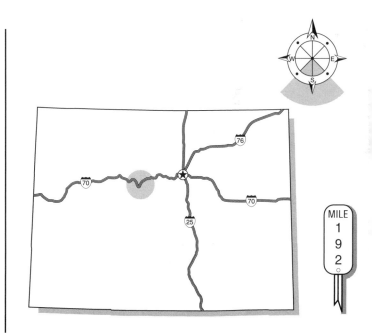

This beautiful panorama is seen by looking to the southeast from the rest stop at the summit of Vail Pass. The elevation at the summit is 10,666 feet above sea level. This view overlooks parts of two Colorado mountain ranges: the Tenmile Range and the Gore Range. Crystal Peak is 8.5 miles away, Copper Mountain is 5.5 miles away, Quandary Peak is 11 miles away, and Jacque Peak is 5 miles away.

Peak 9—13,195 ft. Part of the Tenmile Range, which is actually 12 miles long.

Peak 10—13,633 ft. The tenth peak in the Tenmile Range.

Crystal Peak—13,852 ft. Named after Crystal Creek.

Copper Mountain—12,441 ft. Home of the Copper Mountain ski resort.

Pacific Peak—13,950 ft. This peak sits just west of the Continental Divide.

Quandary Peak—14,265 ft. Miners once found a mineral on the peak that they could not identify. They said they were in a "quandary" to determine what the ore was.

Fletcher Mountain—13,951 ft. Named for a miner by the name of Fletcher.

Union Mountain—12,313 ft. Named for a railway station.

Jacque Peak—13,205 ft. Named for an early prospector who had a mine on the peak.

Jacque Ridge—12,432 ft. Takes its name from Jacque Peak.

Elk Mountain—12,693 ft. Elk are found throughout the Colorado high country.

Sugarloaf Peak—12,545 ft. Sweet-toothed settlers often saw "sugarloaves" in the hills.

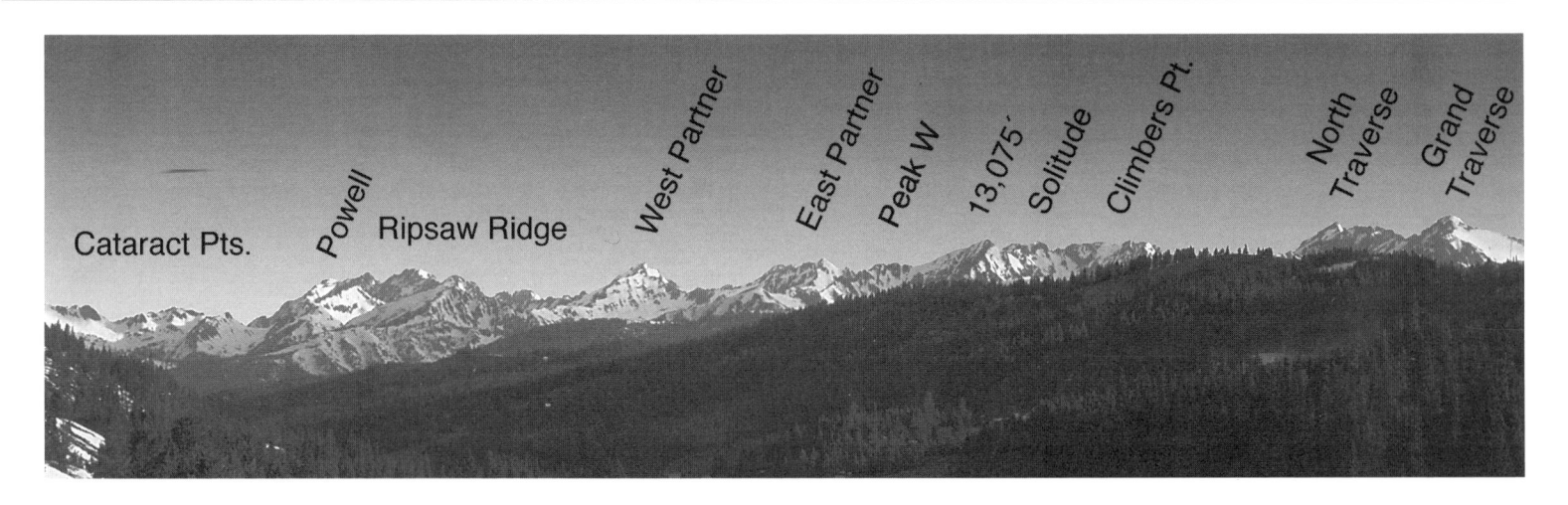

Just north of the Vail Pass summit is a beautiful glimpse of the heart of the Gore Range. Most of these peaks are remote, seldom climbed, and reside within the Eagles Nest Wilderness Area. At one time a custom developed of naming Gore Range peaks after the letters of the alphabet. To this day, most of the peaks have no official name. Mount Powell is almost 17 miles to the northwest.

Cataract Points—12,709 ft. The five high-points on this ridge are known as the Cataract Points:—Pt. 12,709′, Pt. 12,626′, Pt. 12,600′, Pt. 12,663′, and Pt. 12,400′.

Mount Powell—13,560 ft. The highest peak in the Gore Range is named for Major John Wesley Powell (1834–1902), a one-armed Western explorer and geologist. Powell made the first recorded assent of this peak on September 26, 1868. When Powell reached the summit he placed a biscuit and a scrap of paper in a small tin can for whomever might find it in years to come. Later, in 1873 when members of the Hayden Survey climbed the peak for a triangulation fix, they found the rusty old tin can containing an aged biscuit and Powell's writing. The Hayden party decided then and there to name the majestic peak Mount Powell, in honor of the intrepid explorer.

Ripsaw Ridge—13,230 ft. This string of peaks is called the Ripsaw Ridge for its rocky, steep summits similar to teeth on a saw. Peaks C through H are on this ridge.

West Partner—13,041 ft. Also known as Peak U. Neither name is official.

East Partner—13,057 ft. Also known as Peak V. Neither name is official.

Peak W—12,775 ft.   **Unnamed 13,075**—13,075 ft.

Mount Solitude—13,090 ft. Named for its location in the heart of the Gore Range.

Climbers Point—13,005 ft. Named by Bob Ormes, a climber and cartographer.

North Traverse Peak—13,079 ft. Connected to Grand by a steep and narrow ridge.

Grand Traverse Peak—13,079 ft. Named for the prominent connecting ridge.

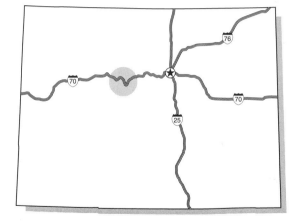

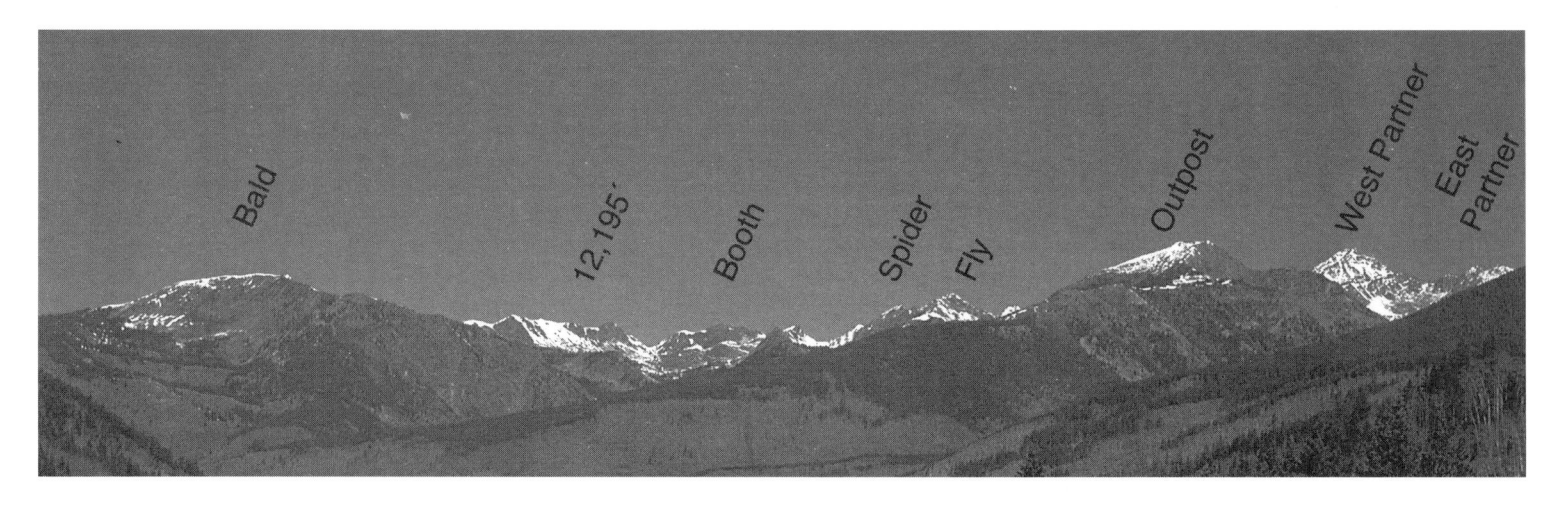

This panorama is viewed by looking northwest to the Gore Range from mile maker 184. Bald Mountain, which is located just north of the east end of Vail, is 6 miles away. Booth Mountain is 7 miles away and West Partner is 7 miles northwest. The Gore Range was previously known as the Blue River Range.

Bald Mountain—12,136 ft. There are 92 mountains in Colorado with the unimaginative word *bald* or *baldy* in their name! Since mountains extending above the treeline are bare or "bald" on their tops, this was a common name to bestow on peaks.

Unnamed 12,195—12,195 ft. The western high-point on along the Booth ridge.

Booth Mountain—12,163 ft. This unofficial name comes from nearby Booth Lake, located at the base of the mountain.

The Spider—12,692 ft. This unofficial name comes from climbers who, in 1962, noted many spiders on the mountain. On arriving at the summit, they spotted a spider web "as big as an umbrella" on the top of this high mountain. The Spider also has many arms or ridges, that spread out like spider legs from the summit.

The Fly—12,560 ft. This peak is so named for its close proximity, and smaller size relative to The Spider.

Outpost Peak—12,362 ft. The prominent south-end peak on this Gore Range spur.

West Partner—13,041 ft. Joe Kramarsic, Gore Range mountain expert, reports that these two peaks, West Partner and East Partner, are named for their close proximity and near identical elevations. These are unofficial names.

East Partner—13,057 ft. The East and West Partner summits are 1 mile apart.

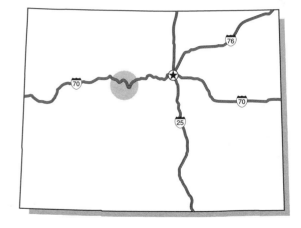

MILE
1
8
4

This panorama, viewed from mile marker 176, is seen by looking towards the east at the white-capped peaks of the Gore Range as they look down on the east end of the Vail Valley. Grand Traverse Peak is almost 6 miles east. Climbers Point is 5 miles away. All of these peaks are located in the Eagles Nest Wilderness Area.

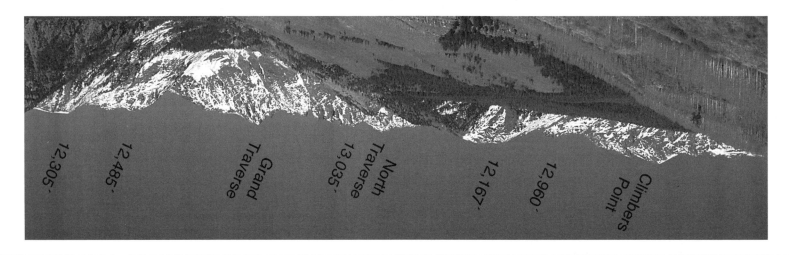

12,305'

12,485'

Grand
Traverse

North
Traverse
13,035'

12,167'

12,960'

Climbers
Point

Climbers Point—13,005 ft. Named by Bob Ormes, a climber and cartographer.

Unnamed 12,960—12,1960 ft.

Unnamed 12,167—12,167 ft.

North Traverse Peak—13,079 ft. The northern point of the Grand Traverse Ridge. The distance along the ridge is 0.8 miles long.

Unnamed 13,035—13,035 ft. The high-point on the ridge between Grand Traverse and North Traverse.

Grand Traverse Peak—13,041 ft. Grand Traverse and North Traverse peaks are the two end points of a dramatic ridge that separates the mountains. No doubt, climbers traveling across these toothy and dangerous crags have a grand experience!

Unnamed 12,485—12,485 ft.

Unnamed 12,305—12,305 ft.

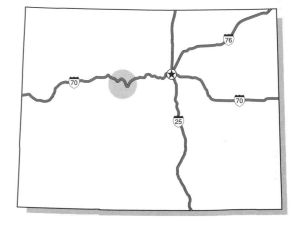

Gore Range mountain names—For some reason, perhaps because of their remoteness, many of the peaks in the Gore Range were never named. As time went by and enthusiastic climbers began exploring and climbing these rugged peaks, names were needed to identify the mountains. Climbers decided that in the absence of names, they would assign letters of the alphabet to the peaks on the range crest and high tributary ridges.

From the town of Vail, at mile marker 175, this panorama is seen by looking east toward Vail Mountain and the world-famous ski resort. Vail Mountain is 3.5 miles away. Before development in the late 1950s, this lovely valley was a sheep pasture.

Vail Mountain—11,250 ft. Vail Mountain takes its name from the town of Vail, which in turn takes its name from Charles D. Vail, chief engineer of the Colorado highway department. Before the ski resort was developed, there was nothing here but a sheep pasture. When the name Vail Pass was applied to the old Black Gore Pass, just a few miles east of town, this location then became known as the Vail Pass area.

The town of Vail was established in 1959. Surprisingly, Vail Mountain is the only named peak in the area, and this name wasn't established until after the founding of the Vail ski resort. Because of the nonsignificance of the area prior to the resort, no names were bestowed on any of the nearby peaks or summits.

Although there are only a couple of named peaks nearby, there are many named bowls and basins on the maps around Vail Mountain. These bowls, which are depressions or basins between the many hills and ridges around Vail Mountain, are an important part of what makes skiing here world class. The bowls are only visible from higher up on the mountain.

Vail ski area—Vail is a world renown ski resort. Hundreds of million-dollar homes are located here. It's hard to believe that when the land was purchased for Vail Village in the late 1950s the land was bought for only 110 dollars per acre!

Vail receives an incredible average of 28 feet of snow per year!

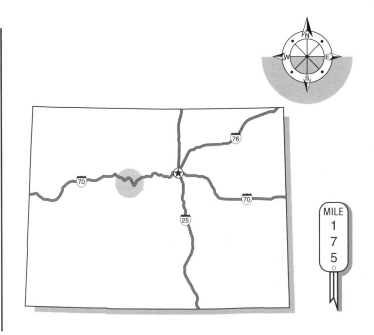

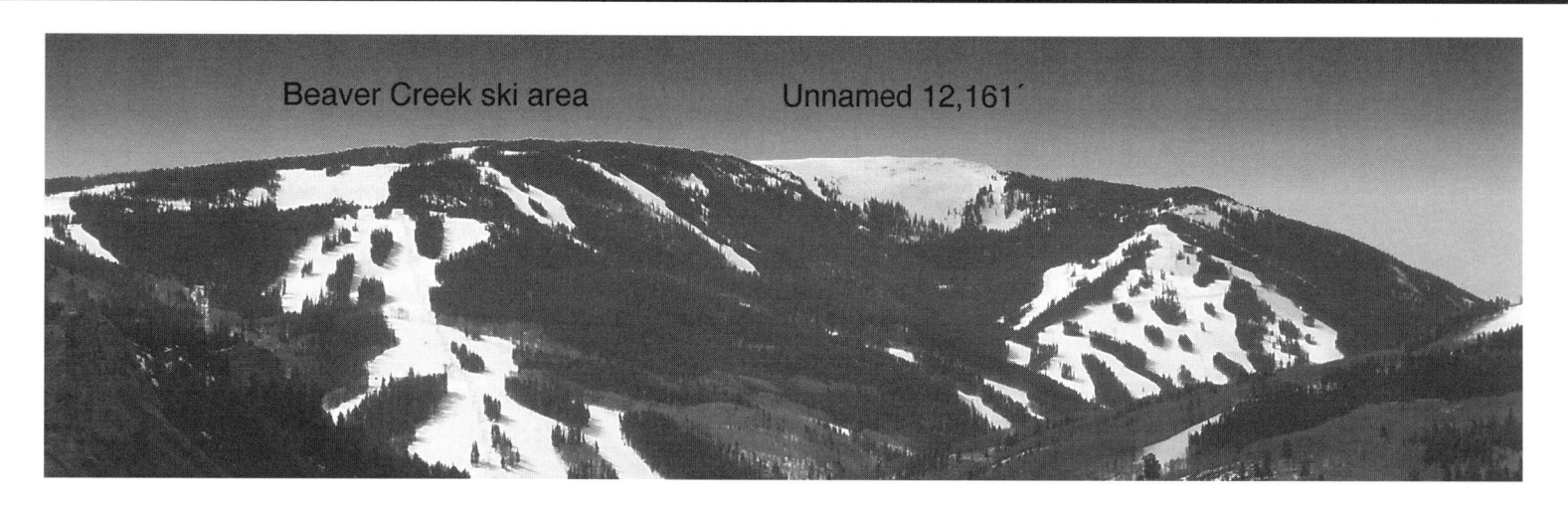

This panorama, from the Avon exit near mile marker 166, can be seen by looking south to the Beaver Creek ski area. The creation of this ski resort was based on Colorado hosting the 1976 Winter Olympic games. Although voters vetoed that plan, Beaver Creek Resort survived and is today a popular, winter and summer resort destination.

Beaver Creek ski area—12,161 ft. Beaver Creek is named for a little stream that flows down from the beautiful Holy Cross Wilderness area to join the Eagle River, near the interstate. The creek is about 8 miles long. As you can imagine by the name, beaver lived along the little stream, which they dammed, creating small lakes.

Before the 1970s and the construction of the Beaver Creek ski resort, this area and Avon were just small hamlets. None of the summits were ever named. The creation of the ski resort caused considerable controversy that took most of the 1970s to resolve. Today, it is a popular winter sports destination.

Unnamed 12,161—12,161 ft. Just over the top of this peak, 5.5 miles south, is Mount of the Holy Cross and many other peaks of the Sawatch Range.

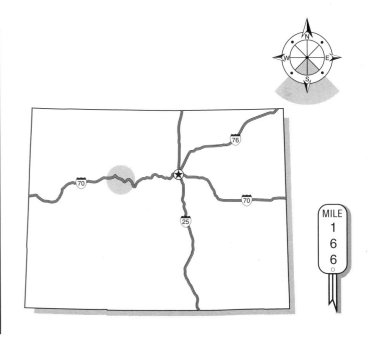

Lionshead—If you look south around exit 171, the Minturn exit, you will see an outcrop of rocks high on the hillside—this is Lionshead. The hillside and the outcrop make up the lions head. See if you can see the lion.

Top of the Rockies—The Top of the Rockies Scenic and Historic Byway bypasses the segment of Interstate 70 between the Minturn exit at mile marker 171, and the Copper Mountain and Leadville exit at mile marker 195. The historic byway is 49 miles long and crosses Tennessee Pass (10,424 feet) and the higher Fremont Pass (11,316 feet). The byway runs through the historic mining town of Leadville, which is at an elevation of 10,152 feet. It's a beautiful drive.

From the scenic pullout at located near mile marker 162, between the towns of Edwards and Eagle, look south to New York Mountain. While it looks like a much shorter distance, New York Mountain is actually 14 miles away. Note: This scenic pullout is on the Interstate 70 eastbound side only.

Unnamed 12,782—12,782 ft. This peak is part of the Sawatch Range.

Unnamed 12,765—12,765 ft. Beyond this mountain is Gold Dust Peak.

Unnamed 12,525—12,525 ft. One of several high-points on the New York Mountain summit ridge.

Unnamed 12,475—12,475 ft. Local residents call these mountains collectively "the New York Mountains."

New York Mountain—12,550 ft. The exact naming of this peak appears to be lost in history. A better-known mountain called New York Peak is located about 37 miles south of this one, near the town of Aspen, and is named for the New York mine, a rich producer in its day. This New York Mountain is not named for a mine. Perhaps a lonely prospector from New York named it to remind him of his faraway home.

The Sawatch Range—Sawatch is from the Ute Indian word *sagwāch,* which roughly translates "blue-green water of the earth." The Sawatch Range is one of the larger ranges in Colorado, stretching 100 miles from the Eagle River, which parallels Interstate 70, south past U.S. Highway 50 and Monarch Pass, all the way to Marshall Pass. The range contains hundreds of peaks and fifteen summits above 14,000 feet! The Continental Divide runs along the range for approximately 75 miles.

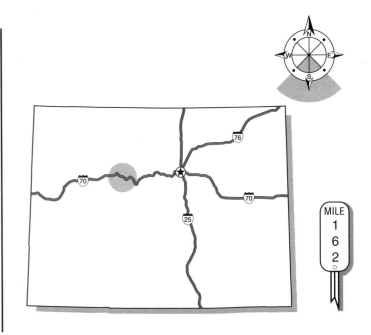

This panorama is viewed by looking to the east-southeast from the Eagle exit, at mile marker 145. These mountains are part of the Sawatch Range. New York Mountain is 15 miles away. Gold Dust Peak is 19 miles southeast. These peaks lie within the Holy Cross Wilderness area.

Unnamed 12,755—12,755 ft. Since all of the peaks listed here are located in the Holy Cross Wilderness area, no new names can be added. Current federal policy forbids new names for features in designated wilderness areas.

Unnamed 12,782—12,782 ft. This ridge connects south to Gold Dust Peak.

Unnamed 13,320—13,320 ft. A high-point on the New York summit ridge.

New York Mountain—12,550 ft. Local residents refer to these mountains collectively as "the New York Mountains."

Unnamed 12,475—12,475 ft. A high-point on the New York summit ridge.

Unnamed 12,525—12,525 ft. Isolated New York Lake sits at the foot of this peak.

Gold Dust Peak—13,365 ft. Gold mining and prospecting were once common in this rough and mountainous terrain. The name Gold Dust Peak may attest to the fact that gold was indeed discovered somewhere on the mountain. Gold Dust Peak is also an enticing and enchanting name for a mountain.

Unnamed 12,911—12,911 ft. High ridges radiate in all directions from Gold Dust Peak, like gigantic arms of a petrified starfish.

Unnamed 13,126—13,126 ft. A high-point on a Gold Dust ridge top.

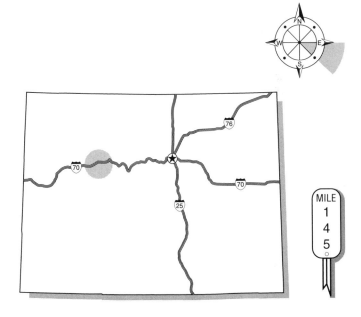

These two pictures show Castle Peak from exit 157 and exit 145. The photo on the left is from exit 157, the Wolcott exit. The picture on the right is from exit 145, the Eagle exit. Notice how much the view of the peak changes in just 10 miles. From exit 157 we see Castle Peak, edge on, while from exit 145 we see the complete side of the mountain. Castle Peak is about 9 miles away in both photos.

Castle Peak—11,275 ft. Named for its resemblance to a castle—remote, isolated, and perched high on a hill. It was most likely named by the Hayden Survey in the 1870s. This peak has also been known as Courthouse Peak. *Castle* is another common name for many mountains and rocky crags across Colorado.

Glenwood Canyon—About 12 miles west of Eagle, Interstate 70 enters Glenwood Canyon. Although there are no named features in Glenwood Canyon, the sheer beauty of the canyon and the remarkable highway design deserve a few words.

Glenwood Canyon begins at mile marker 131 and follows the meandering Colorado River for 18 miles through Glenwood Canyon to the town of Glenwood Springs, Colorado. The futuristic freeway looks down on the Colorado River as it winds its way through the canyon. Smoothly sweeping curves and high-tech tunnels carry motorists through the canyon with minimal disturbance to the beauty and nature that abounds between its sheer, rocky walls. A bike path also winds along the riverbank of the mighty Colorado River.

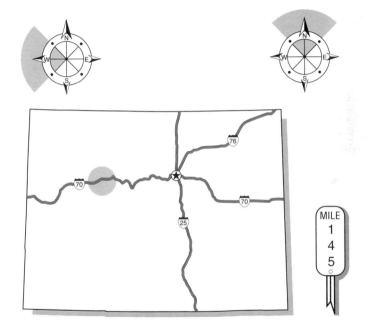

Glenwood Springs to Grand Junction

This photograph was taken by looking southeast to the mountains at mile marker 115. Mount Sopris is a conspicuous landmark in the Glenwood Springs and surrounding areas. You must look quickly to see it from here, as the surrounding hills and trees block the view of the impressive peak from most positions along the interstate. Mount Sopris is 22 miles to the southeast. Mount Richey is 32 miles away.

Unnamed 12,164—12,164 ft. One of the high-points close to Mount Sopris.

Mount Sopris—12,953 ft. Named for Captain Richard Sopris (18??–1893), who explored the area in 1860. After spotting the mountain, Sopris announced that he would ride his faithful mule, Jerry, to the top of the mighty peak. Some distance up the mountain, in deep snow, old Jerry laid down and refused to budge. Captain Sopris, believing his old friend had exhausted himself and would surely die, retreated down the mountain, forlorn over the loss of his good mule. That night, while the captain and his men sat around the campfire, old Jerry lumbered into camp none the worse for wear. Right then and there, the members of the party decided to name the peak Mount Sopris for the incident involving their leader.

West Sopris—12,953 ft. The westerly summit of Mount Sopris.

Mount Richey—12,240 ft. This mountain is named for a man by the name of Richey who was a long time forest service worker in the area.

Unnamed 12,973—12,973 ft. A "third-order" permanent benchmark on the top of this peak is known as "Hawk." Benchmarks are precisely positioned markers that are used by surveyors and cartographers. Thousands of them exist throughout the country. They are often identified by a round brass disk cemented in place at the benchmark location. Benchmarks measure horizontal position and/or elevation and are rated for accuracy. They are constructed and maintained by the USGS.

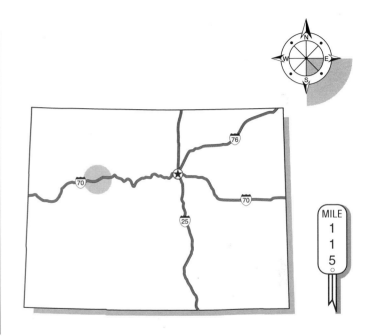

These two photographs are taken from the west end of Glenwood Springs from two locations between mile marker 112 and mile marker 115. Looking to the east, you can see Lookout Mountain 5 miles away. Looking west, Storm King Mountain is visible on the outskirts of Glenwood Springs, 3 miles farther west, near exit 111.

Storm King

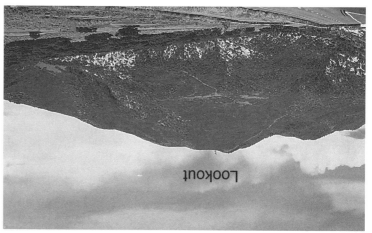

Lookout

Lookout Mountain—8,643 ft. A forest lookout tower is located on the summit, which may have led to the name of this peak.

Storm King Mountain—8,793 ft. This mountain has been known as Storm King Mountain for many decades. On July 6, 1994, Storm King Mountain once again earned its name when a raging fire storm swept through South Canyon and Storm King Mountain taking the lives of fourteen firefighters. Smoke jumpers had flown in from around the country to help extinguish the sweeping forest inferno. A rapid shift in wind direction caught fourteen men and women on a ridge of Storm King where they lost their lives. The names of the fallen firefighters are:

Kathi Beck—Eugene, OR	Tami Bickett—Powell Butte, OR
Scott Blegha—Clatskanie, OR	Levi Brinkley—Burns, OR
Robert Browning—Savannah, GA	Doug Dunbar—Redmond, OR
Terri Ann Hagen—Prineville, OR	Bonnie Holtby—Prineville, OR
Jon Kelso—Prineville, OR	Don Mackey—Grand Junction, CO
Rob Johnson—Redmond, OR	Roger Roth—McCall, ID
James Thrash—McCall, ID	Richard Tyler—Grand Junction, CO

A trail now leads through the charred remains of tree stumps to a memorial located at the top of the peak. The memorial is dedicated to the brave men and women who gave their lives on the now infamous Storm King Mountain.

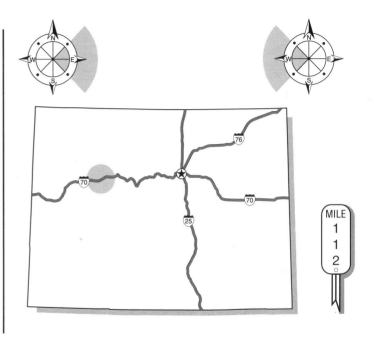

GRAND HOGBACK

Coal Ridge

The gigantic Grand Hogback begins a few miles west of Glenwood Springs. It runs in a long arc almost to Meeker, a distance of about 50 miles. This east-facing picture is taken from the overpass at the New Castle exit, mile marker 105.

Grand Hogback—7,254 ft. A hogback is a geologic feature that is formed when the caprock tilts at a steep angle to the underlying bedrock. More than a dozen formations in Colorado are called the Hogback.

Bedrock is the underlying, unweathered rock beneath the surface soil. Bedrock consists of layers of rock called *beddings* that have been laid down over eons. The caprock is a hard rock that is more resistant to erosion than the softer rock below it. This can often lead to different rates of erosion, which create many of the buttes and mesas we see today.

Tilting of the layers of bedrock happens over the millennia. Different pressures within the earth and along the earth's crust cause the bedrock to buckle, fracture, and split. Sometime they rise to tremendous heights, creating hills or mountains.

The road crosses Grand Hogback which continues west and can then be seen to the north of the interstate. The high-point on the Grand Hogback, 8,973 feet, is located farther along the hogback, south of Meeker, Colorado.

Coal Ridge—7,665 ft. Many parts of the Grand Hogback contain large coal deposits. Old coal mines can be found along this ridge.

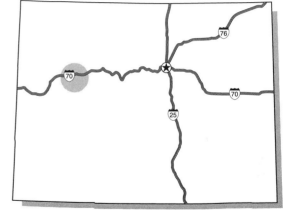

From mile marker 97 near Silt, look to the southwest to Battlement Mesa, which dominates the skyline. It is 14 miles away. Nearby Weible Peak is 1.5 miles to the southwest. North Mamm Peak is 16 miles from the interstate.

Weible Peak—5,911 ft. Probably named for an early settler in the area.

Battlement Mesa—11,123 ft. Named by the Hayden Survey because the mesa has a notched top resembling the parapets along the top of castle walls.

North Mamm Peak—11,123 ft. Just over the top of Battlement Mesa lies North Mamm Peak. Farther to the southwest is South Mamm Peak. North Mamm Peak is the high-point of Battlement Mesa.

North Mamm and South Mamm refer to breasts, or mammary glands. The peaks are recorded in the Hayden Survey of 1877, indicating they are quite old names. Puritanical settlers tried to hide this fact by referring to the peaks as Mamma Peak or Mam Peak, instead of Mamm Peak. Father Escalante tried to name them San Silvestre, for North Mamm, and Nebuncari, for South Mamm, but these names never stuck.

There are other peaks in Colorado that are named for this portion of the anatomy; The Spanish Peaks, conspicuous southern Colorado landmarks, were known to Native Americans as the *Wa-ha-toy-ah*, meaning "two breasts" or "breasts of the world."

How do you name a mountain?—It has long been customary in the United States to commemorate and perpetuate local or national individuals who have contributed to society by attributing their name to a peak. Today, this is very difficult. Documentation, justification, and strong regional support are needed to receive a positive ruling from the United States Board on Geographic Names.

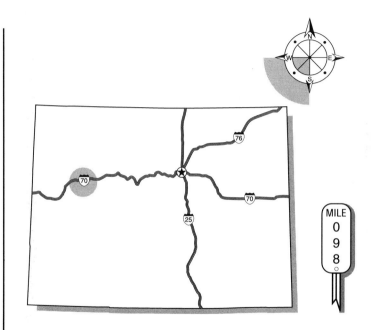

From the Airport Road exit at mile marker 94, the Roan Cliffs take shape on the horizon. The cliffs are about 11 miles away. From this location along the interstate you can see the southeastern corner of the cliffs. They continue northward and westward for many miles.

Devils Park

Roan Cliffs

West Anvil Point
East Anvil Point

West Anvil Point—7,620 ft. (approx.). West Anvil and East Anvil points are also collectively referred to as the Anvil Points. They take their name from a blacksmith's anvil. As you approach them, you will notice that they look like the point end of an anvil.

East Anvil Point—7,600 ft. (approx.). These two points are prominent on the plateau summit of the Roan Cliffs.

Roan Cliffs—9,064 ft. The Roan Cliffs are named for their mix of color—chestnut brown with a sprinkling of whites or gray. These colors are in the clay of the soil on the cliffs. Roan is a common coat color in some horses. The cliffs were described by William Beckwith, a member of the Gunnison expedition, in 1853. Perhaps the cliffs reminded him of the colors of his own roan horse.

Devils Park—8,015 ft. The word *devil* appears in 72 different place names in Colorado. From Devils Slide to Devils Kitchen, the word seems to suggest connotations of heat, bizarre, or twisted shapes, and perhaps fearful heights or places.

What is a park?—The term *park* is used frequently in Colorado and is derived from a French word meaning "enclosure." It usually describes areas such as meadows or valleys that are surrounded by mountains or other such barriers. Examples of parks include Middle Park, South Park, and Woodland Park.

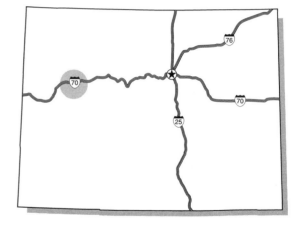

95

GRAND HOGBACK

This panorama is viewed by looking north from mile marker 94 at the Airport Road exit. All along the northern skyline you can see the Grand Hogback. The farther west you go, the farther the distance to the hogback, as it curves in a northwesterly direction. Due north from here, the hogback is about 5.5 miles away.

Grand Hogback—8,973 ft. When caprock tilts at a steep angle to the underlying bedrock, a geological feature called a *hogback* is formed. The Grand Hogback is by far the largest hogback in Colorado, stretching almost 50 miles in length.

The Grand Hogback extends from north of here, close to Meeker, Colorado, and trends in a southeasterly direction, until it reaches the western outskirts of Glenwood Springs.

The Grand Hogback marks the western boundary of the Rocky Mountains in Colorado. As you travel across Colorado on Interstate 70, this bumpy margin defines your entry or exit to the great Colorado Rockies.

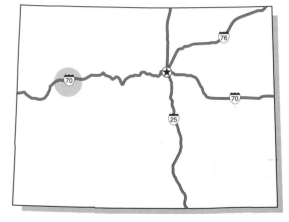

Geographical and historical source information—Since there are sometimes conflicting names, elevations, or origins of place names for some mountains, it can be a challenge to unravel the geographic and historic puzzle that these peaks present. To make matters worse, many geographic terms are relative, such as mountain, hill, river, or range. Many historical names, events, and explanations have never been recorded or perhaps lost in history. All of this adds to the confusion factor when trying to verify or define such things as a mountain name, a boundary, or where something happened. Many of these conflicts still exist. Multiple sources sometimes cite different explanations. The correct conclusions must therefore be left to the reader to ponder and future research to resolve.

These two photographs show the Roan Cliffs from mile marker 83, near the Rulison exit. The photograph on the right is a close-up of the Anvil Points. From this position, the cliffs are about 1 mile from the highway.

Roan Cliffs

East Anvil

West Anvil

Roan Cliffs

Roan Cliffs—9,064 ft. Named for the color of the clays within the cliffs, which are similar to the coat color of a roan horse. On top of the Roan Cliffs is the Roan Plateau. This plateau is hundreds of square miles in size and contains one of the world's largest reserves of energy in the form of coal, shale oil, and natural gas. This arid plateau region, stretching from northwestern Colorado into Utah and northward into Wyoming, is estimated to contain several billion gallons of oil in its sedimentary rock!

The substance in the shale that yields oil is called *kerogen,* a waxy material that, when heated, produces petroleum. In approximately sixty pounds of crushed high-grade oil shale, about one gallon of petroleum can be produced.

Needless to say, to obtain mineral and water rights, oil companies and the U.S. government have purchased considerable land in this area of Colorado. Water is a key ingredient in removing the oil from the shale.

West Anvil Point—7,620 ft. (approx.). West Anvil and East Anvil points are also collectively referred to as the Anvil Points. They take their name from their resemblance to a blacksmith's anvil.

East Anvil Point—7,600 ft. (approx.).

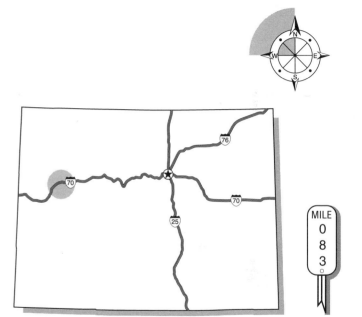

Near the town of Parachute at mile marker 75, this panorama is viewed by looking to the north-northeast. Allen Point is 3.25 miles away. Cottonwood Point is 6 miles away. Both of these mesas are part of the Naval Oil Shale Reserve.

Allen Point—8,532 ft. The exact naming of this summit seems to be lost in history.

Roan Cliffs—9,064 ft. The cost of extracting the highly rich petroleum from the oil shale contained in the Roan Cliffs and surrounding countryside has kept oil companies from disturbing much of this land. In the sad event of an energy crisis, or if a more practical way of removing the oil from the shale is developed, much of this virgin landscape would be extensively mined.

Cottonwood Point—7,670 ft. Cottonwood Point takes its name from Cottonwood Gulch, which contains Cottonwood Creek. The gulch is located to the left, or west side, of Cottonwood Point.

The cottonwood is a prolific tree that grows along riverbanks and fertile bottom lands in Colorado. It grows up to 100 feet tall and provides cool shade.

Genesis, Adam, and the naming of the land—Which landmarks are named and which are not named often depends a lot on *who* the settlers and local residents were. Some seem to have been direct descendants of Adam, naming every prominent and not so prominent protrusion, peak, and point as far as the eye could see. In other areas, there's hardly anything named, which reflects the quiet, reserved character of those early residents.

This panorama looks south from mile marker 69, between the towns of Parachute and De Beque. Horse Mountain is 7.5 miles to the southwest, Housetop Mountain is 7 miles away, Castle Peak is 10 miles southwest, and Horsethief Mountain is 9.5 miles distant.

Horsethief

Castle

Housetop

Horse

Horse Mountain—9,289 ft. Wild horses once roamed this area, which led to the name of this mountain. There are thirty summits in Colorado named *horse*.

Housetop Mountain—8,297 ft. If you use your imagination, you might see that the hump on top of this peak resembles a crude house. This series of bumps was at one time known as the Housetop Mountains.

Castle Peak—8,302 ft. Another common name for a mountain. There are twenty seven landmarks in Colorado with the word *castle* in the name.

Horsethief Mountain—7,844 ft. In the early West there was no lower form of life than a yellow-bellied horsethief! After being caught, horse thieves were often hanged on the spot. The exact reason for the naming of this peak appears to be lost in history. The name certainly suggests that some kind of incident took place on or near this mountain. Perhaps it's somehow related to Harvey Logan (see Mount Logan, next page). Logan and his accomplice stole horses in the area for their getaway. Possibly it was near this mountain.

How far can you see?—On flat ground, on a clear, sunny day, you can only see about 2.5 miles before the curvature of the earth blocks your view. However, if you are at a higher elevation looking down, or looking at a taller object such as a mountain, you could see more than 100 miles.

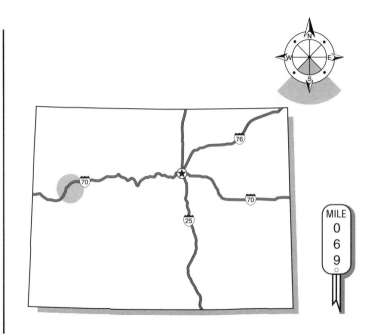

These two lonely, barren peaks are located to the north of Interstate 70, between the towns of De Beque and Parachute. This panorama is viewed by looking north to Mount Logan and Mount Callahan from the Garfield-Mesa County line, at mile marker 65. Mount Logan is 2 miles away. The summit of Mount Callahan is 6 miles north.

Mount Logan—8,413 ft. Mount Logan is named for Harvey Logan, a.k.a. "Kid Currey." Logan and his brother were members of the infamous "Hole-in-the-Wall gang" that included "Butch" Cassidy and the "Sundance Kid." This group, which was known as the "Wild Bunch," had a notorious reputation. Logan, who may have been the most despicable outlaw of the lot, was reputed to have shot forty-one men. Logan and two associates came to Parachute on June 7, 1904, to rob the Denver & Rio Grande #5 train of $150,000 in gold bullion. Through an inept mistake, *they robbed the wrong train.* After using twice the dynamite necessary to open the safe, and blowing a large part of the railcar to pieces, they made their escape on horseback. With a posse in hot pursuit, they stole fresh mounts as they escaped. The posse finally cornered the outlaws and a gun battle ensued. When the smoke cleared, one bandit was dead and two escaped. Pinkerton detectives identified the body as Harvey Logan. He is buried in Glenwood Springs, Colorado not far from "Doc" Holiday.

Mount Callahan—8,606 ft. This peak commemorates an early Parachute resident—Mike Callahan. In 1882, Mike built a nice log cabin complete with a beautiful fireplace constructed of the plentiful slate-colored shale that could be found locally. After his hard work, Callahan invited his friends and neighbors over for a housewarming. With a roaring fire burning in the new fireplace, it looked like the party would be a great success, when suddenly the chimney burst into flames, burning the house and all of Mike's possessions and proving once again what the local Ute Indians had known for many years; the strange, blue-gray rock would burn! Mr. Callahan went on to become a lifelong advocate of oil shale, predicting a rich future for it.

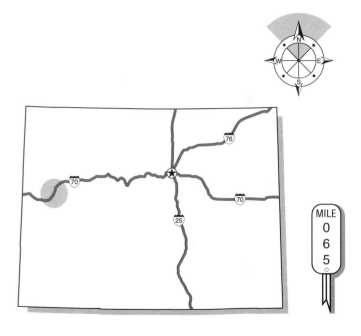

105

From mile marker 61, located 1 mile west of De Beque, this picture was taken by looking to the southwest to Grand Mesa about 16 miles in the distance. The flat top of the mesa covers more than 50 square miles and is known as the world's largest flat-topped mountain. Local residents describe it as the 10,000-foot island in the sky.

Grand Mesa—11,086 ft. Grand Mesa takes its name from the Colorado River, which was originally known as the Grand River. Early explorers and settlers named the majestic mesa "Grand," a title befitting this imposing landmark along the mighty Grand River. Grand Mesa is visible from as far west as the Colorado-Utah border and south of Delta.

Sprinkled over the summit of this naturally formed *mesa*, which is Spanish for "table," are more than two hundred lakes. The mesa is covered with lush forests of pine and is thick with wildlife. The Ute Indians called it *Thigunawat*, meaning "home of departed spirits" or "the happy hunting ground."

The Utes also had a legend about how the Grand Mesa came to be: Giant thunderbirds called *Bahaa-Nieche* nested on the summit of the great plateau. The white rocks below the cliffs were the bleached bones of the thunderbirds' prey—deer, antelope, and Indian children. One day a *Bahaa-Nieche* carried off the son of a great chief to the top of the mountain and fed the poor boy to its young. The father, seething with rage, disguised himself as a cedar tree and began to scale the side of the mesa. If a *Bahaa-Nieche* flew overhead, the chief would freeze and appear to be just a another tree. When the angry father reached the summit, he took all of the great birds' young and flung them off the mesa into the jaws of a giant snake that lived at the foot of the mesa. The *Bahaa-Nieche*, on their return to their nests, finding their young eaten, fell into a rage and immediately sought out the snake. Lifting the snake high into the air, the great birds pecked and pulled the giant snake into small pieces. As they fell, they formed craters on the mesa's summit and created the many lakes we see today.

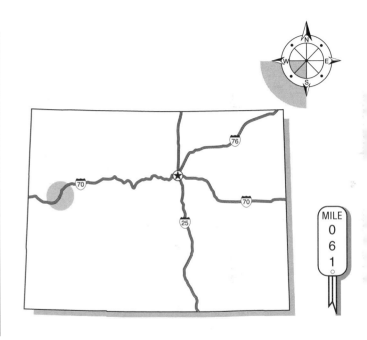

This photograph, taken from mile marker 60, east of De Beque Canyon, is a westerly view of the barren, desolate hills of the Colorado plateau region. The Twin Peaks are 7.5 miles west and Horse Mountain is 14 miles away. Pyramid Rock is nearby at 3 miles and the prominent Cow Ridge is 11 miles away.

South Shale Ridge—8,022 ft. Much of the surrounding countryside is made up of shale, including energy-rich oil shale. The estimates of the amount of shale oil contained within the region range from several billion to almost two trillion barrels!

Twin Peaks—7,442 ft. Named for the two summits that are located near one another. The Twin Peaks mark the eastern edge of South Shale Ridge.

Horse Mountain—8,482 ft. Also known as Horse Ridge. This ridge is 10 miles long.

Pyramid Rock—5,540 ft. As the name suggests, this peak resembles a pyramid.

Cow Ridge—8,476 ft. On first thought, Cow Ridge seems to be named for the bovine with which we are all so familiar. However, this may not be the case, as many different female mammals are known as cows, including the female buffalo.

De Beque Canyon—Just west of mile marker 60, Interstate 70 follows the Colorado River into and through De Beque Canyon. De Beque is named for an early settler to the area, Dr. Wallace de Beque. The canyon is about 10 miles long and follows the bends of the Colorado River. There are only two named features in the canyon: Beaver Tail Mountain and Long Point. They are easily spotted from the interstate. De Beque Tunnel passes through Beaver Tail Mountain, and the road makes a very long, sweeping curve around Long Point. You can see Long Point from mile marker 53.

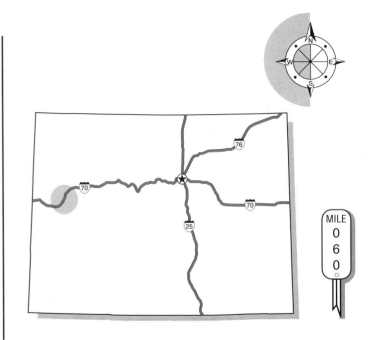

Mount Lincoln

Mount Lincoln and nearby Mount Garfield, which is located just 3 miles west of Lincoln (you can't see it in this photograph), are both named for assassinated U.S. presidents. This panorama is viewed by looking northwest from the Cameo exit at mile marker 44, to Mount Lincoln, 2.5 miles northwest. Surprisingly, the large bluff to the right has no name.

Mount Lincoln—6,649 ft. Named in memory of the sixteenth U.S. President, Abraham Lincoln (1809–1865). Lincoln was mortally wounded by a gunshot on April 14, 1865, at Ford's Theatre, Washington, D.C.

How do you name a mountain?—It has long been customary in the United States to commemorate and perpetuate the memory of local or national individuals who have contributed to society by attributing their names to peaks. Today, this is very difficult to do. Documentation, justification, and strong regional support are needed to receive a positive ruling from the United States Board on Geographic Names.

How you can help protect the mountains—Today, with more and more people visiting our mountain and wilderness areas, erosion, trash, and pollution can all be by-products of visiting these natural wonders. Lean how to have minimal impact and protect and conserve these delicate ecosystems. Practice low-impact hiking and "leave no trace" camping. Support conservation efforts to preserve and protect our wilderness lands. No matter what your interest in the mountains are; there is an organization which you can support in preserving *our* land for generations to come. Some of these organizations include the National Parks Foundation, the Sierra Club, the Colorado Mountain Club, and the Audubon Society. Get involved!

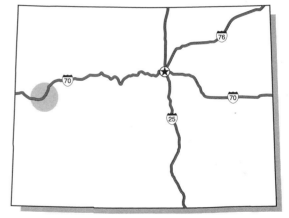

This panorama looks south from mile marker 43. Below, the green and fertile fields of Palisade can be seen. Behind, rise the Book Cliffs and Mount Garfield. The well-proportioned mesa known as Horse Mountain is about 3 miles away.

Horse Mountain—5,988 ft. Although the name of this summit is Horse Mountain, it is more correctly described as a mesa. The naming of this distinguished rock is not known. What a thrilling sight it would be to see a wild mustang prancing proudly on the summit.

Wild horses—The wild horses of the West are now actually descendants of horses belonging to early explorers, Native Americans, and cowboys. After escaping captivity they eventually gathered in herds. In the early 1900s there were more than 2 million wild horses, called *mustangs,* wandering the West. Most were captured and killed for pet food. Today there are fewer than 20,000 wild horses roaming the West. In Colorado, there are only a few mustangs, located about 100 miles north near Craig.

How a mesa is formed—The Colorado River, over the millennia, quietly but efficiently eroded the surrounding soft shale and sandstone, while the lava-capped rock of the mesa resisted erosion. Wind and rain also helped to erode the softer rock. The result is the steep-sided feature we see today.

This panorama is viewed by looking north from the scenic pullout located at mile marker 38. Mount Garfield is 1.5 miles to the north. The Book Cliffs run from Mount Garfield, west, in a large semicircle, as far as the eye can see.

Book Cliffs—6,765 ft. The Book Cliffs received their name because of the distinct layers of sandstone and shale that can be seen on the cliff sides. Using your imagination, the cliffs look like piles of books stacked up on the valley floor.

The Book Cliffs cover a distance of 60 miles, running from Palisade, west into Utah. They mark the northern end of the Grand Valley, making a huge semicircle around its northern edge. The high-point on the cliffs is Mount Garfield at 6,765 feet.

Mount Garfield—6,765 ft. Named in honor of President James A. Garfield (1831–1881), who was assassinated shortly after taking office in 1881. Several Colorado geographic features are named after the twentieth U.S. president.

Mount Garfield and the Book Cliffs have a cap of erosion-resistant rock called the *Mesaverde* caprock. Where this resistant roof is missing, the underlying soft, loose, shale erodes easily, causing the mountainsides to crumble. This gray and yellow soil does not readily support the growth of vegetation, and thus the cliffs are barren and empty, resembling a lunar landscape.

Mount Garfield rises 2,000 feet above the surrounding Grand Valley floor.

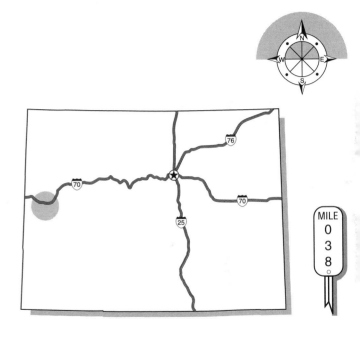

This panorama shows Monument Canyon from the Book Cliffs overlook, in Colorado National Monument, not far from the monument visitor center on the west side of the national monument. The Monument Canyon floor is several hundred feet below the overlook. Independence Monument is about 1 mile east.

Monument Canyon—Monument Canyon received its name because it's the main canyon in the Colorado National Monument. The canyon is about 5 miles long and has a wonderful trail that winds its way along its bottom.

Wedding Canyon—John Otto married Beatrice Farnham at the bottom of Independence Monument in June 1911, which led to the name.

Kissing Couple—5,815 ft. These fractured, red stone pinnacles stand together, barely touching, in an eternal kiss. They are approximately 400 feet high.

Independence Monument—5,739 ft. The most prominent pillar in Colorado National Monument is Independence Monument.

Pipe Organ—5,731 ft. Using your imagination, you can see the gigantic pipes and reeds of a red rock pipe organ. The Pipe Organ formation is about 400 feet tall.

Praying Hands—5,700 ft. (approx.). This pillar, seen from many directions in the canyon, looks like two clasped hands with the fingertips pointed skyward.

Wet Weather—During infrequent heavy rains, the monument comes alive as the runoff forms rivulets. Waterfalls of beautiful red and chocolate browns cascade down the canyon walls—a sight not to be missed!

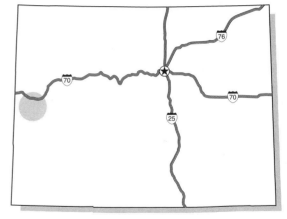

This panorama shows Monument Canyon from the Monument Canyon overlook, located inside Colorado National Monument. This view is located several miles east of the monument visitor center. Photography of the canyon is best in the early morning when the low angle of the sun enriches the canyon colors.

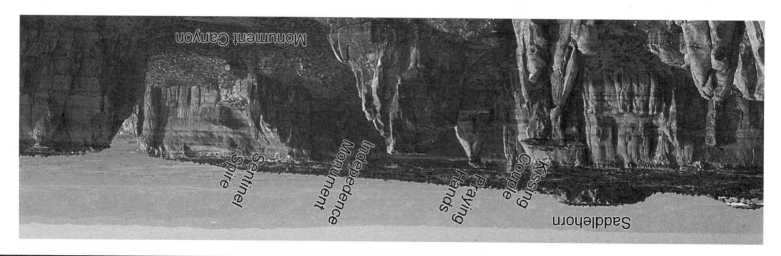

The Saddlehorn—5,849 ft. Named for its resemblance to the leather knob on the front of a western saddle called a *saddlehorn*. This rock is about 50 feet in height.

Kissing Couple—5,815 ft. Two red stone pinnacles stand together, barely touching, in an eternal kiss. This pinnacle is about 400 feet tall.

Praying Hands—5,700 ft. (approx.). From this overlook you can see the two praying hands, palms together with fingertips pointed skyward, which led to this pillar's name. The hands are approximately 400 feet tall.

Independence Monument—5,739 ft. The most prominent pillar in Colorado National Monument, this huge sandstone monolith (which is 450 feet tall) was so named because it was first climbed by John Otto on July 4, 1910. Otto erected a flag on the summit of the monument commemorating Independence Day. Local residents still scale the peak each fourth of July to raise the American flag, celebrating American independence. Otto also carved a portion of the Declaration of Independence into the side of the rock. John Otto and his young bride, Beatrice Farnham, were married at the bottom of Independence Monument on June 20, 1911. Two months latter, Beatrice left John and never returned.

Sentinel Spire—5,300 ft. (approx.). This lonely stone pillar "guards" the north entrance to Monument Canyon—hence its name. It is about 250 feet high.

Monument Canyon—The main canyon at the Colorado National Monument.

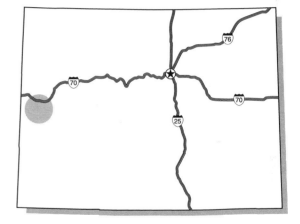

This panorama is viewed by looking south of Interstate 70 from between Fruita and Grand Junction. You can see the northeastern edge of the great Uncompahgre Plateau. Contained along the northern edge of the plateau is the Colorado National Monument, 4 miles away.

Colorado National Monument—4,700 ft. to 7,028 ft. (approx.). The Colorado National Monument covers an area of 32 square miles, approximately 20,000 acres of beautiful canyons, red-hued spires, and sandstone monoliths. Rim Rock Drive, 23 miles long, runs from Grand Junction and Fruita, Colorado, carrying visitors through the magnificent canyons and overlooks. The monument visitor center is located on the Fruita side, or west end, of the monument.

Because of the untiring work and single-handed efforts of John Otto, Colorado National Monument was officially dedicated and opened in 1911. Otto became the park's first superintendent. An eccentric individual by anyone's account, he came to Fruita, Colorado, in 1907 and fell in love with these red rock canyons. He built many of the roads and trails in the monument and originally wanted to name it *Smith Monument* figuring that Smith was such a common name that Smiths from around the country would visit the park and ensure its success. Thankfully (no offense to the Smiths), this name was dropped in favor of Colorado National Monument.

Uncompahgre Plateau—13,144 ft. Covering much of southwestern Colorado, the Uncompahgre Plateau stretches southward for more than 100 miles. Millions of years ago, part of the Ancestral Rocky Mountains, known as the *Uncompahgria Range*, was located in the same general area as the present-day Uncompahgre Plateau. This portion of the plateau is characterized by red sandstone, hard caprock, and sedimentary layers. *Uncompahgre* is a Ute Indian word roughly meaning "hot-water spring."

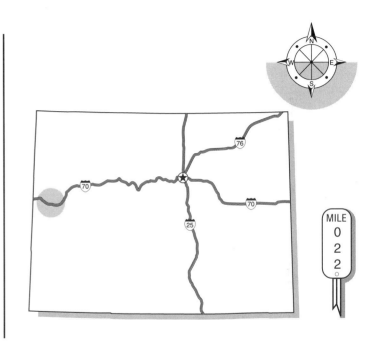

Index

LOOK FOR THESE UPCOMING PEAKFINDERS GUIDEBOOKS!

PeakFinders Guide to Hwy. 550, Durango to Ouray

PeakFinders Guide to Hwy. 160, Durango to I-25

PeakFinders Guide to Hwy. 50, Pueblo to Montrose

FALL '97

PeakFinders Guide to Hwy. 24, Colorado Springs to Leadville

SPRING '98

OTHER PEAKFINDERS GUIDEBOOKS:

PeakFinders Guide to the Colorado Mountains Interstate 25 Skylines

Joe Milligan is a writer, digital photographer, and Colorado mountain expert. He is the author of two books and a member of the Colorado Mountain Club, the International Association of Panoramic Photographers, the Colorado Historical Society, and the Colorado Independent Publishers Association.

Joe is available to present a free slide show to organizations or clubs about the majestic Colorado mountains. Contact him via the publisher or send E-mail to peakfinders@usa.net